1992 AND ALL THAT

1992
AND ALL THAT

CIVIL LIBERTIES IN THE BALANCE

Michael Spencer

The Civil Liberties Trust

The Civil Liberties Trust
21 Tabard Street
London SE1 4LA

British Library Cataloguing In Publication Data

Spencer, Michael
1992 And All That: Civil Liberties in the Balance
1. Civil rights. Effects of integration of
European Community countries. European Community
countries. Integration. Effects on civil rights
1. Title II. Civil Liberties Trust
323.094

ISBN 0-900137-34-7

The Trust's publications do not necessarily reflect the views of the Trust.

Designed by Jeff Sanders, Edward Bear Associates, London.
Typeset in Stempel Garamond and ITC Garamond.
Printed on recycled paper by Crowes, Norwich.

Contents

Preface

I first became aware of the civil liberty implications of '1992' when I worked on an earlier project for the National Council for Civil Liberties (Liberty) concerning identity cards in Britain. One of the arguments used by their proponents was that, with the proposed abolition of internal frontiers by the end of 1992, identity cards would have to be introduced throughout the European Community. Whether this will happen remains to be seen; the point is that a domestic issue like this can no longer be considered in isolation from the situation elsewhere.

In pursuing this topic I learnt some interesting things about the differences between European countries - not only in their laws, but in the attitudes of both governments and individuals towards a given issue concerning civil liberties. I was therefore very glad to be offered an opportunity to explore the effects of the 1992 process - both positive and negative - on a much wider range of issues.

It would not have been possible to write this book without help from a wide range of experts in each of the areas covered. At official levels I received invaluable assistance from both civil servants in Britain and European Commission staff in Brussels; they answered innumerable questions, explained their policies, and supplied documents of whose existence I had been unaware. The Commission also made the whole project viable by giving a grant towards the cost to the Civil Liberties Trust.

At a non-government level I received similar assistance and great encouragement from a large number of organisations and individuals, who not only supplied information but drew attention to the potential dangers to civil liberties in each area. Last but not least, library staff at the London offices of the European Commission and the European Parliament were unfailingly helpful.

As the book neared completion, a number of individuals other than staff from Liberty and the Civil Liberties Trust kindly agreed to read particular chapters and provide expert opinions: they were John Alderson, Tony Bunyan, Colm Campbell, Patrick Canavan, Stewart Dresner, Don Flynn, Avis Furness, Jeanne Gregory, Alain Guyomarch, Howard Machin, Nuala Mole, Robert Reiner, Tony Venables and Lord Wedderburn of Charlton. The book is undoubtedly better for their advice, but of course any errors or omissions are my own.

Within Liberty and the Civil Liberties Trust I have of course had unstinting help from everyone, particularly Madeleine Colvin (Legal Officer), Renée Harris (Publications Editor), Chris Jones (Librarian), Fiona McElree (Campaigns Officer) and Alison Vickers (Women's Rights Officer). Paul Hunt (now with the United Nations) kindly contributed much of the material for Chapter Six. Malcolm Hurwitt and Christine Jackson, two trustees of the Civil Liberties Trust, also made comments on the final draft. Finally, Francesca Klug (Director of the Civil Liberties Trust) not only contributed material on the democratic deficit (Chapter One) but supervised the whole project with unfailing good humour and an experienced eye for detail during the drafting process.

It only remains to add that in referring to the notes at the end of each chapter, I have followed the science-based convention on which I was nurtured: where a cross-reference is needed to an identical citation earlier in the same chapter, the original number is repeated to refer the reader directly to that note.

Michael Spencer
August 1990

About the Author

Michael Spencer is a former Senior Research Fellow in science at Kings College, London, who has worked since 1984 as a writer and researcher for campaigning groups on third world development and civil liberties issues. He has previously written for Liberty on identity cards and video surveillance in public places.

Glossary

The list below contains only the most common terms, particularly those which create confusion between the European Community (EC) and the Council of Europe. For page references to fuller definitions, and for Council of Europe terms not listed here, see the Index. For an explanation of more than 500 terms, see also: Stephen Crampton, *1992 Eurospeak Explained* (Rosters, 1990).

Commission (European Commission)
: Executive body of the EC, composed of 17 commissioners appointed jointly by member states.

Committee of Ministers
: *Council of Europe* body comprising the foreign ministers of member states and their deputies.

Communication
: A formal submission from the *Commission* of the EC to the *Council* of the EC, presenting a report or setting out its future intentions.

Convention
: An international treaty between states, drawn up *either* between EC states *or* by member states of the *Council of Europe*.

COREPER
: Committee of *Permanent Representatives* of the member states of the EC.

Council (Council of Ministers)
: Legislative body of the EC, composed of representative ministers from member states.

Council of Europe
: 23-nation organisation set up in 1949; quite separate from the EC.

Decision
: Binding decision or instruction issued by the *Council* of the EC on a topic for which a *Directive* or a *Regulation* is inappropriate – for instance, an instruction to a particular company or individual.

Directive
: Binding instruction issued to all EC states by the *Council*, directing them to introduce national legislation in a given area.

European Commission of Human Rights
Council of Europe institution which investigates cases brought under the *European Convention on Human Rights.*

European Convention on Human Rights
A *Convention* drawn up by the *Council of Europe* and ratified by all EC states.

European Council
Meeting of EC heads of government and others in a 'summit'.

European Court of Human Rights
Council of Europe institution which decides cases brought under the *European Convention on Human Rights.*

European Court of Justice
EC institution charged with ensuring that Community law is observed.

European Parliament
EC parliament of elected members.

Memorandum
A document similar to a *Communication* from the EC's *Commission* to the EC's *Council*, raising a new issue for discussion.

Opinion
Formal view on a draft proposal, issued by the *Commission* or by the *European Parliament* of the EC.

Parliamentary Assembly
Council of Europe parliament of members nominated by national parliaments.

Permanent Representatives
In the EC, national representatives of ambassador status who assist members of the *Council.* In the *Council of Europe*, the deputies of the foreign ministers of member states.

Qualified majority
Majority vote in the *Council* of the EC, weighted according to the size of population of the member state.

Recommendation
Issued *either* by the *European Commission* of the EC *or* by the *Committee of Ministers* of the *Council of Europe.* The *Parliamentary Assembly* of the

latter body also issues Recommendations to the Committee of Ministers of the Council of Europe.

Regulation
Binding regulation issued to all EC states by the *Council* or by the *Commission*. Unlike a *Directive*, it has immediate effect without the need for national legislation.

Resolution
Issued *either* by the *Council* of the EC *or* by the *Committee of Ministers* of the *Council of Europe*. In the latter case they were called *Recommendations* from 1979 onwards.

Third country national
Citizen of a non-EC state.

Main institutions of the EC and the Council of Europe

The list below compares institutions whose composition and function are *roughly* similar in each case; their actual powers are not at all comparable.

European Community	*Council Of Europe*
European Parliament	Parliamentary Assembly
European Council Council [of Ministers]	Committee of Ministers
European Commission	Council of Europe Secretariat
European Court of Justice (Community law in general)	European Court of Human Rights (human rights only)

INTRODUCTION
Who Stands To Gain?

What has '1992' got to do with civil liberties? On the positive side, quite a lot, if you happen to be a woman hoping for greater equality at work, better maternity and childcare benefits, or more protection against sexual harassment; or if you happen to be a worker wanting better consultation with the management of a firm before major decisions are taken. These are some of the potential benefits of the process that began with the signing of the Treaty of Rome in 1957. This established a European Community (EC) in which there would be not only freedom of movement, but also equality of opportunity, and improved living and working conditions for all.[1]

The Single European Act of 1986 gave new urgency to the process of change, with the declaration that the Community should aim to create an 'area without internal frontiers' by 31 December 1992.[2] The Act also encouraged further moves to improve the working environment and 'develop the dialogue between management and labour at European level', and this led in 1989 to the Social Charter – controversial among politicians and employers in Britain, but broadly accepted elsewhere in the Community.

However, the emphasis of most EC legislation has always been on the *economic* benefits of closer integration; the Single European Act specifies the need for freedom of movement for 'goods, persons, services and capital' as a means of 'progressively establishing the internal market'. Apart from the principle of equal treatment for women (enshrined in the original Treaty of Rome), there has until recently been little consideration of the broader issues of human rights and civil liberties within the Community.

There is therefore a danger that in the rush to 'harmonise' (i.e. equalise) the Community's laws and regulations, some groups in society may actually be disadvantaged unless proper safeguards are put in place. Even in a positive initiative like the Social Charter there are notable omissions; there is, for instance, only the most general declaration against racial discrimination – at a time when many see an alarming increase in racism and fascism in some parts of Europe.

A further danger lies in what is arguably an obsessive fear among EC governments of perceived threats from outside the borders, and alarm about a possible explosion of international crime when internal frontier controls are relaxed. As a result of measures taken in response to these fears, 1992 could, for example, adversely affect a genuine refugee trying to enter Europe; an immigrant resident in Europe, seeking to cross internal borders in search of work; a black or ethnic minority citizen of an EC state, harassed by the police as a suspected illegal immigrant; or anyone whose name has got into a computerised government or police file as a political activist.

It is in this respect that the prospect of '1992' evokes for some an unfortunate echo of George Orwell's *Nineteen Eighty-Four*, in which he describes a totally enclosed and regulated society – one of three world superpowers, called Oceania – that is indifferent or actively hostile to all nations outside it; a society turned in on itself, in which the authorities watch and control everyone in the name of Big Brother. Nobody would wish the European Community to travel down that road, but some groups in society fear that it may.

This book surveys the likely impact of the 1992 process on a wide range of civil liberties. While drawing on examples from other EC countries, it is primarily concerned with the possible or likely effects of the changes on the UK and on Community institutions as a whole. It examines both sides of the 1992 coin – the dangers as well as the benefits for civil liberties. It also takes account of the exciting political developments of the end of 1989 and the first half of 1990, with the possibility of a dramatic widening of the Community to include at least some of the new Eastern European democracies. Political union, too, is now being canvassed as never before; as this book was being written, issues were being raised in public debate that fifty years ago were no more than dreams in the minds of a few far-thinking idealists. If there has been a need to project and speculate at times in these pages, this is because new developments will certainly occur even as we go to press.

Chapter One starts by explaining some of the complex workings of the EC and the respective role, power and status of the European Commission, the Council (or Council of Ministers), the European Council (when heads of government meet in a 'summit'), and the European Parliament. The important influence of the older and quite separate Council of Europe on the EC is discussed. Attention is also focused on the inter-government committees of EC ministers and officials which meet in secret – outside the framework of Community institutions – and which have already made far-reaching decisions affecting all of us: the Trevi Group, the Working Group on Immigration, and the cryptically named Co-ordinators' Group.

The so-called 'democratic deficit' – the failure of the Community to ensure full accountability to European electors – is also considered in Chapter One. This is seen most starkly in the inability of the European Parliament – which is the only EC institution directly elected by the people of Europe – to exercise any real control over the many important decisions made by the Commission and Council, not to mention those made by completely unaccountable bodies like the Trevi Group. Most EC governments acknowledge that this will have to change. The British Government, however, is opposed to giving the European

Parliament more legislative powers, and generally refuses to accept the argument that crucial features of the current constitutional system are undemocratic.

Other nations in the Community take a different view, and are anxious to talk further about political union between states. They see this as a logical and necessary consequence of all the Community treaties that have so far been signed – by Britain among others. The issue is discussed here without advocating any specific constitutional arrangement, the point being that full civil liberties demand a more democratic and accountable political structure for the Community than that which currently exists.

The work of the Trevi and other groups on external border controls and policing (*Chapter Two*) reflects the preoccupation of EC governments with the spectre of external threats: they deal with asylum-seekers and would-be immigrants from the Third World as 'problems' on a par with terrorists, international criminals and drug-traffickers. The decisions made to date reflect the increasingly hostile view taken by many EC governments of those rejected as 'economic migrants', and follow the precedent already set by the Schengen Agreement and Convention between five of the EC states.

The decisions now being taken on immigration and visa policy could seriously undermine the Geneva Convention on the treatment of refugees, and lead to increased harassment of black and ethnic minority people already living in the Community; they are likely to have their citizenship or immigration status questioned even more frequently than is currently the case. Unless the underlying attitudes are changed, it is likely that immigration controls will be 'harmonised downwards' towards the most restrictive policies now practised among member states – an outcome completely at variance with the spirit of the Treaty of Rome.

Chapter Two also shows how the Community, while giving freedom of movement and social benefits to its own citizens, has done virtually nothing for the many people who live and work in the Community but who do not have citizenship of an EC state. These 'third country nationals' are likely to become increasingly underprivileged, and open to all forms of exploitation. The European Parliament, which opposes these trends, has no power to intervene; the issue is held to be outside the scope of Community treaties.

Chapter Three deals with another source of concern – the area of data protection, including the preservation of individual privacy where personal details (involving such matters as political opinions) are recorded in a file. Should such details be freely circulated between government agencies (including the police and security forces) throughout the Community? Could trade union activists find themselves victimised all over the Community because their file has been passed between companies? Will refugees find that their relatives at home have been persecuted because of information leaking back from Europe? The emphasis has so far been on encouraging the free circulation of information, and only now are Commission officials drawing up rules to place limits on this flow. Should there be a supranational Commissioner for Data Protection to supervise the transmission of data across borders? We show why this may be needed.

A related issue is that of identity cards. Some politicians claim that the abolition of border controls will make inevitable their introduction into countries like the UK and the Netherlands which do not currently have them; that they are already accepted throughout most of Europe, and that the law-abiding individual has nothing to fear from them. None of these statements is true. Furthermore, a national identity card might well be linked with a national registration number which could ultimately be used by any official (or even private) agency to follow the movements of an individual – something with far-reaching implications for civil liberties.

This issue overlaps that of police powers (*Chapter Four*) in a more integrated Community. What powers would the police or security forces of one state have to cross into another and operate there? Will there be pressure for a Community police force? If so, to whom would it be accountable? These questions have barely been raised – and have particular relevance to Britain, where there is widespread unease about the current system of police accountability. Co-operation in the field of criminal justice (particularly extradition) is also discussed; this is another area where harmonisation could erode safeguards against errors and miscarriages of justice.

On the more positive side, *Chapter Five* deals with the Social Charter and discusses the problems of implementing it. The British Government was the only one to vote against the final Charter in December 1989, and many of its key proposals could still be blocked by a British veto. Britain has already stalled previous moves to give workers a greater say in the running of their firms – yet works councils on which employees sit are a standard feature in many European countries. On almost every aspect of 'social Europe' Britain is resisting the current trend, or is even moving backwards towards the nineteenth century. Commission surveys and other reports indicating the extent of this problem are quoted.

Chapter Six goes on to deal with the protection of basic human rights in a Community preoccupied with economic issues, and with the power to override national legislation in certain areas. Surely the liberties of the citizen should be given equal protection in every member state? This question involves two issues. Firstly, in the context of harmonising other laws it would make sense (for instance) for the Community to accede to the Council of Europe's European Convention on Human Rights. This has already been proposed by the President of the European Commission, Jacques Delors. The possibility of political union (see below) would provide a further incentive for the formulation of a Community-wide standard for basic civil liberties, by following up accession with a specific Community Bill of Rights.

Similar arguments apply at a national level. Why, at present, should it be necessary for an individual to work through all the courts of the British system before reaching the European Court of Human Rights in Strasbourg? A simple answer – advocated by many groups in Britain including the National Council for Civil Liberties (Liberty) – is for the European Convention to be incorporated into our law, so that any domestic court could give effect to it in judging a case.

The book ends in *Chapter Seven* with a summary of the issues. A list of relevant campaigning organisations, and some information on Euro-lobbying, are given in two of the appendices. Original sources are listed at the end of each chapter for those wishing to pursue a given topic further.

In conclusion, it should be said that this is not a campaigning book, though certain preferences will no doubt become apparent. Its purpose is to present information covering a wide range of civil liberty issues arising out of the 1992 process; to assess the balance between gains and losses for civil liberties; and finally to make suggestions for tilting the balance towards the gains. It is for campaigners and policy-makers to argue about ways and means of achieving this. One thing, though, is clear: on the basis of experience to date it would be unwise to leave the protection of civil liberties to concerned politicians or individual governments alone. The debate will need to be taken up by the general public – the many millions of ordinary people whose lives will be affected by the changes now under way.

Notes

1. The terms 'Community' and 'European Community', and the abbreviations EC or EEC, are commonly used to refer to the European Economic Community, established by the treaty signed in 1957 and generally called the Treaty of Rome. Strictly speaking there are three Communities involving the same member states, although they now share a common structure. Earlier treaties had set up the European Coal and Steel Community (signed 1951) and the European Atomic Energy Community (1957); hence the plural form in the *Official Journal of the European Communities*, frequently cited in this book. For the basic text of the treaties (including changes later made in them) see *Treaties Establishing the European Communities*, abridged edition (Office for Official Publications of the European Communities, Luxembourg, 1987).
2. Cm. 372 (HMSO, London, 1988); also *Official Journal of the European Communities*, L169 (29 July 1987).

CHAPTER ONE

How The European Community Works

The way the European Community operates is obscure to many people. Understanding is not helped by the fact that many of the titles of Community institutions – the Commission, the Council, the European Court and so on – partly duplicate those of different institutions belonging to the older, and quite separate, Council of Europe. The latter will be referred to quite often in this book because of its profound influence on Community practice and law-making. This influence becomes even more important now that the Community is turning its attention to topics such as data protection and human rights legislation, where the Council of Europe has long ago set precedents. It is as well to start, therefore, with an explanation of the structures of these two different bodies.

The role of the Council of Europe

Set up in a spirit of great optimism in 1949, the Council of Europe was created as a meeting-point for all the pluralist democracies of Europe. It was intended to heal the rifts between nations left by the Second World War, and was established as a result of a specially convened Congress of Europe in 1948 which strongly endorsed the idea of an ultimate European Union. It was at this Congress that the proposal for a Convention on Human Rights was also launched.[1]

Based in Strasbourg, the Council of Europe currently has 23 members; in addition to those nations which also form the EC (Belgium, Denmark, France, West Germany, Greece, Ireland, Italy, Luxembourg, the Netherlands, Portugal, Spain and the UK) it also includes Austria, Cyprus, Finland, Iceland, Liechtenstein, Malta, Norway, San Marino, Sweden, Switzerland and Turkey.

The scope of the Council of Europe's remit is broad, covering human rights, social rights, legislation and judicial procedures, culture, youth, education and training, health, the environment, the media, local democracy, and sport; defence, however, is not included. It has a *Parliamentary Assembly* of 177 members (with an equal number of 'substitutes') appointed by national parliaments, to which about 50 parliamentary watchdog committees and sub-committees report on each area of interest. There are also guest delegations to the Parliamentary Assembly from Hungary, Poland, the Soviet Union and Yugoslavia; Czechoslovakia and Bulgaria are expected to follow. The Assembly has three week-long sessions a year for debates; however it has no legislative or executive power.

The executive body is the *Committee of Ministers*, made up of the Foreign ministers of member countries or their deputies (the *Permanent Representatives*). It meets twice yearly, but there are also monthly meetings of the ministers' deputies. There is also a *Joint Committee of Ministers and Representatives of the Parliamentary Assembly*, the only formal link between the two institutions. The Council of Europe also has a Secretary General and over 900 staff, who among other things service more than 120 inter-governmental committees.

Since only the Committee of Ministers has executive power, the decision-making process is simple. On the basis of reports which it receives, the Committee adopts detailed *Conventions* and *Agreements* which are then open for signature and ratification by member countries; these are international treaties, regarded as binding once they are ratified. A country can, however, enter a derogation, reserving the right not to comply with certain parts of such a treaty. This small print is sometimes the most significant part of the document, which may otherwise consist of broad declarations which nobody would dispute.

The Committee of Ministers also issues formal *Recommendations* (called *Resolutions* before 1979), as well as *Declarations* on matters of principle. Some of these documents have been widely influential; for instance, Recommendation R (87) 15 on the use of personal data used by the police has recently been adopted as an international standard, both by the signatories of the five-nation Schengen Convention (see Chapter Two), and by the interior ministers of the EC states meeting in the Trevi Group (see Chapters Two and Three).

By far the best known of the 130 Conventions and Agreements so far produced by the Council of Europe is the *European Convention on Human Rights*, which all EC countries have both signed and ratified (the formal step needed to bring it into effect). This is considered in detail in Chapter Six; at present the European Community, by contrast, has no formal structure of its own for considering human rights, other than a small unit in the Secretariat-General which has a remit covering the rest of the world as well.

Under the Convention on Human Rights, the Strasbourg-based *European Commission of Human Rights* of legal experts considers each complaint about a breach of the Convention and decides whether it is admissible; it then tries to achieve a friendly settlement between the complainant and the relevant member state. If this is not possible, it makes a formal report to the Committee of Ministers. From here, during a period limited to three months, the Commission of Human Rights and/or the state or states concerned can pass the case to a second body appointed as judges, the *European Court of Human Rights* (also in Strasbourg, and not to be confused with the UN's International Court of Justice at the Hague, nor with the European Court of Justice at Luxembourg – for which see below). The European Court of Human rights is involved if an important question of law needs to be considered. If the Court is not asked to consider the case, the Committee of Ministers makes a decision subject to a two-thirds majority vote (see below).

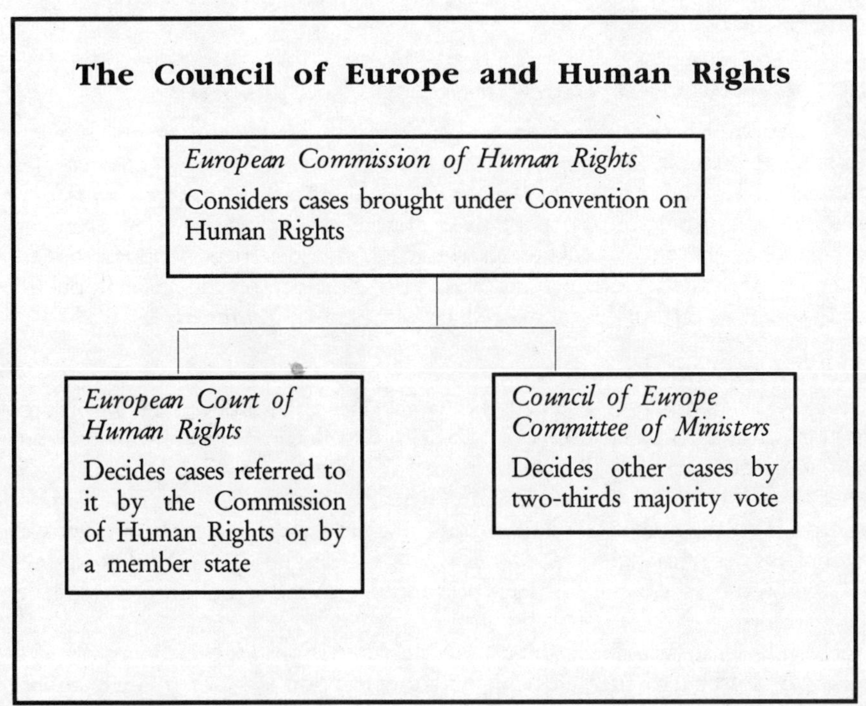

Other Council of Europe Conventions to which we shall refer are those on data protection (Chapter Three), extradition (Chapter Four), and mutual assistance in criminal justice (Chapter Four). There is also a European Social Charter which predates the more recent Community Social Charter (Chapter Five). Several Council of Europe Recommendations relating to data protection are listed in Chapter Five, and these will acquire extra relevance as the European Community develops its own policy in this area.

Unlike the European Community, the Council of Europe is not limited in its scope by detailed terms of reference like those in the EC's Treaty of Rome (see Introduction). The Treaty acknowledges the importance of this unrivalled source of expertise in Article 230, which states: 'The Community shall establish all appropriate forms of co-operation with the Council of Europe'.

Despite its invaluable work in many fields, however, the Council of Europe has failed to live up to the hopes of at least some of its founders; it never acquired the power to make new laws, and the decisions of the Committee of

Ministers are limited by the need in practice to obtain unanimous agreement. It has thus been unable to fulfil the original intention of moving towards political union between members, and in this respect it has been overtaken by the European Community.

The structure of the European Community

The Treaty of Rome specifies four institutions to implement its provisions: a *European Parliament*, a *Council*, a *Commission* and a *Court of Justice*. The Council and Commission are to be assisted by an advisory *Economic and Social Committee* consisting of 'representatives of the various categories of economic and social activity, in particular... producers, farmers, carriers, workers, dealers, craftsmen, professional occupations and representatives of the general public'. Financial matters are to be monitored by a *Court of Auditors*.[2]

The European Parliament

Although the European Parliament heads the list of institutions in the Treaty, this does not at present reflect its ability to influence decisions. It is quite different from national parliaments in that its function is largely consultative (rather like the House of Lords in Britain), though it can make minor adjustments to the budget. In cases of fundamental disagreement its only ultimate sanctions are to refuse approval of the whole Community budget, or to dismiss the Commission as a body. The first power, but not the second, has occasionally been exercised.

The European Parliament holds full public sessions in Strasbourg (like its Council of Europe counterpart), but its administration is based in Luxembourg and its specialist committees meet mostly in Brussels, where the European Commission is based. The Parliament has 518 members, of which 81 come from the UK. It meets for a five-day session in every month except August, but with an extra session in October to discuss the Community Budget. Since 1979 its members have been directly elected, and the Single European Act gave it greater powers than it had at first (see below); the members, however, remain very dissatisfied with their role in determining Community legislation.

The Council

The Council (often called the Council of Ministers) is the *law-making* body of the Community, and it reflects the interests of the national governments of member states in the decision-making process. Unlike most national legislatures, however, it meets in secret; in this sense it acts more like the cabinet of a national government.

The makeup of the Council varies, depending on the topic under consideration, though there is always one representative from each member state.

Thus agriculture ministers from each country comprise the Agriculture Council, and so on. The so-called 'summit' meetings involve prime ministers (in the case of France, the president), together with their foreign ministers, the president of the Commission and one other Commission member. This grouping (formally constituted under Article 2 of the Single European Act) is called the *European Council*; it currently meets twice a year and is the main forum for discussing broad political issues. There is also provision (under Article 236 of the Treaty of Rome) for calling an inter-governmental conference on any issue requiring amendment of the Treaty.

These various manifestations of the Council approve, modify or reject proposals put forward by the Commission, with the European Council (the 'summit') having the last word on some issues. There is also an intermediate body called the *Committee of Permanent Representatives* (COREPER), comprising member states' ambassadors to the EC; it considers proposals on their way to the Council and does much of the day-to-day bargaining between member states. If agreement is reached here, a measure is usually adopted without further debate by the appropriate Council.[3]

This mode of operation has been described in a quotation from a former British Permanent Representative as follows: 'In one sense, COREPER and the Council together are a forum for a permanent negotiation between member governments... In another, they are the legislature of the Community. In another, they are the senior board of directors...'[3] This description of COREPER's role is somewhat grander than that defined by the Treaty of Rome, which speaks only (in Article 151) of 'preparing the work of the Council and... carrying out the tasks assigned to it by the Council'.[4]

The Council cannot in general act without receiving a proposal from the Commission, though it can ask the Commission to study an issue and draw up proposals. It can also adopt a non-binding Resolution of its own (see below) as a call for further action by the Community, for instance on a proposal by the current president.

The presidency of the Council rotates between countries every six months. Thus in the second half of 1990, Italy will take the chair at each Council meeting. It is common for each country to attempt to make its mark during the short period of its presidency, by bringing forward those proposals which it favours.

The Commission

The Commission is, broadly speaking, the *executive* body of the Community. It initiates legislative proposals which are put to the Council, and when the Council makes a decision it supervises the implementation of the agreed policy. It is charged with ensuring that the provisions of the Treaty of Rome are implemented, and that proposals for action under the Treaty are formulated; it also has some powers of independent action (see below).

The Commission consists of 17 members of all 12 nationalities, appointed by joint agreement between member governments and serving for renewable four-year terms of office. Members are, however, pledged to remain independent of their national governments – an arrangement which has produced a certain coolness between some British nominees and their government on the grounds that they have become too European-minded.

The president of the Commission and six vice-presidents are chosen from within the Commission for renewable two-year terms, again by agreement between member states; the president cannot therefore be compared to a directly-elected president or a prime minister. Each commissioner is allocated an area of special responsibility. Commission staff are organised into a secretariat-general and various directorates-general (DGs). The ones most relevant to this book are DG III (covering the internal market and harmonisation of laws), DG V (employment, social affairs and education) and DG XIII (telecommunications, including data protection).

It will already be clear that the Commission is not a civil service in the British sense, since it is not under the direct control of elected politicians. The Commission can, in fact, take a member state before the European Court of Justice (see below). It can investigate complaints against a member state from any quarter, including individuals. In recent years the Commission has spent an increasing proportion of its time considering representations from the European Parliament, even though that body has few powers of coercion. This function gives the Commission a democratic legitimacy that it otherwise lacks; it effectively acts as a channel of communication (albeit with a degree of filtering) between the elected Parliament and the Council.

The Court of Justice

The European Court of Justice is based in Luxembourg and comprises 13 judges. It considers both actions brought by the Commission against member states, and actions against the Commission itself by member states and individuals. The Court is the final arbiter on the interpretation of the Treaty of Rome and other Community treaties; its procedures are similar to those in national supreme courts (in Britain, the House of Lords).[4] Because of its increasing workload, the Single European Act authorised the creation of a *Court of First Instance* to hear cases brought by individuals and 'legal persons' (e.g. companies), and this was agreed in July 1988; it delivered its first judgment in January 1990.[5] There is still a right of appeal on a point of law to the European Court of Justice.

The European Court of Justice is now often called upon to rule on questions referred to it by national courts. Community law is increasingly interwoven with national laws, as mandatory provisions of the Treaty of Rome and subsequent Community decisions are incorporated into national laws. An individual can bring an action in a national court and cite a provision of the Treaty of Rome, for instance Article 119 which requires men and women to receive equal pay for equal work. Where there is doubt concerning the consistency of national and Community laws in such a case, the European Court can be asked to give a preliminary ruling by the highest national court. The result may well be that the national law has to change.

A recent ruling by the European Court of Justice which excited controversy in Britain was the decision (in a case over fishing rights) that an injunction be granted in a British court to suspend the operation of an Act of Parliament, pending full adjudication on whether the Act contravened Community law. British courts have not previously had this power, though it is accepted in other countries such as West Germany and the USA.[6]

Decision-making in the Community

The Council and the Commission (and in some areas the Commission alone) can, after going though the proper procedure, issue a range of pronouncements which have different and well-defined effects, most of which are specified in Article 189 of the Treaty of Rome:

- *Regulations* are binding in their entirety and are immediately applicable to all member states. The Commission can issue these on its own where they involve the implementation of 'secondary legislation', i.e. laws based on the Treaty of Rome in an area such as the Common Agricultural Policy.
- *Directives* are also binding, but the method of achieving the result (e.g. by introducing or amending national legislation) is left to each member state.
- *Decisions* (not subsequently referred to in this book) can be binding instructions issued to a particular government, enterprise or individual. They can also announce a change in the composition of the Community, as when a new member is admitted. A Decision was issued to establish the Court of First Instance (see above).
- *Recommendations* and *Opinions* (issued by the Commission) are not binding.
- *Resolutions* are not specified in the Treaty and are also non-binding. The Council can issue a Resolution to put an issue on the agenda for

discussion by governments, or to endorse a Communication from the Commission (see below).

- *Communications* and *Memoranda* are issued by the Commission to raise issues for discussion by the Council, in advance of any formal proposal for legislation.

The first stage in formulating most of these documents is for Commission staff in the appropriate directorate-general to submit a draft to the Commission. If the Commission approves (if necessary by a simple majority vote), the proposal is put to the Council and officially published (see Appendix IV). It has been known for details to emerge unofficially at an earlier stage.

A great deal of preliminary bargaining goes on over which form of pronouncement should be issued, particularly over whether it should be a binding Directive or a non-binding Recommendation. Unless the Commission is authorised to act alone, the final decision rests with the Council.

Council voting procedures

Under the Treaty of Rome, most Council decisions during the period 1958-65 had to be unanimous. There was supposed to be a move to majority voting in 1966, but this provoked an internal crisis which threatened to break up the Community. The result was the 'Luxembourg compromise', an informal understanding giving a member state the right of veto where 'very important interests' were involved.[7] This definition is clearly open to abuse, and for some time it restricted the scope of new initiatives by the Community. The underlying dispute remains unresolved, as shown by the British Government's reluctance to cede any more sovereignty to a more powerful Community structure (see below).

The Single European Act attempted to overcome this problem by specifying a range of topics where 'qualified majority voting' would apply. Under this system, voting is weighted according to population. France, Germany, Italy and the UK have ten votes each; Spain eight votes; Belgium, Greece, the Netherlands and Portugal five each; Denmark and Ireland three each; and Luxembourg two. Out of the total of 76 votes, 54 are required for a qualified majority. Since the introduction of the Single European Act, the 'Luxembourg compromise' has never been resorted to for matters covered by the Act – though the British Government still reserves the right to use it.

Although the change to qualified majority voting has helped, it has not proved a complete answer to the problem. Disputes between member states and the Commission now centre on which article in the Treaty of Rome is the appropriate basis for a given measure – one requiring unanimity, or one allowing a qualified majority vote. The underlying questions, central to the philosophy and operation of the Community, remain unresolved: to what extent should the interests of one member be sacrificed to the greater interest of the majority? And can the interests of a member state in any case be adequately represented by one minister who, as we shall see, is in practice barely accountable to his or her national Parliament on EC matters?

Consultation with the European Parliament

Before the Single European Act introduced a new 'co-operation procedure', the European Parliament's role was purely consultative. Once approved by the Council, a proposal would be sent to both the Parliament and the Economic and Social Committee, which could suggest amendments to the Commission for a revised draft. However, the Council could simply ignore these opinions. This 'consultation procedure' still applies in some areas: broadly speaking, those covering fiscal matters, free movement of labour and measures involving workers' rights.

The new co-operation procedure, on the other hand, involves several additional stages (see diagram overleaf):

- After obtaining the opinion of the Parliament, the Council draws up a 'common position' by a qualified majority which is sent back to the Parliament for a second reading. The Parliament has three months in which to endorse it (expressly or implicitly), reject it or amend it. The Council may then override a rejection, but only by a unanimous vote.
- If amendments have been suggested, the Commission reviews them (within one month) and recommends either acceptance or rejection by the Council. In the case of acceptance, the Council can approve the revised proposal by a qualified majority; if the Commission recommends rejection, the Council may accept or otherwise amend the proposals by a unanimous vote alone.
- If the Council fails to act within three months of receiving suggested amendments (with a one-month extension if agreed by the Parliament) then the proposal lapses, effectively allowing the Council to block any amendment with which it disagrees by simply doing nothing.

The Community legislative process

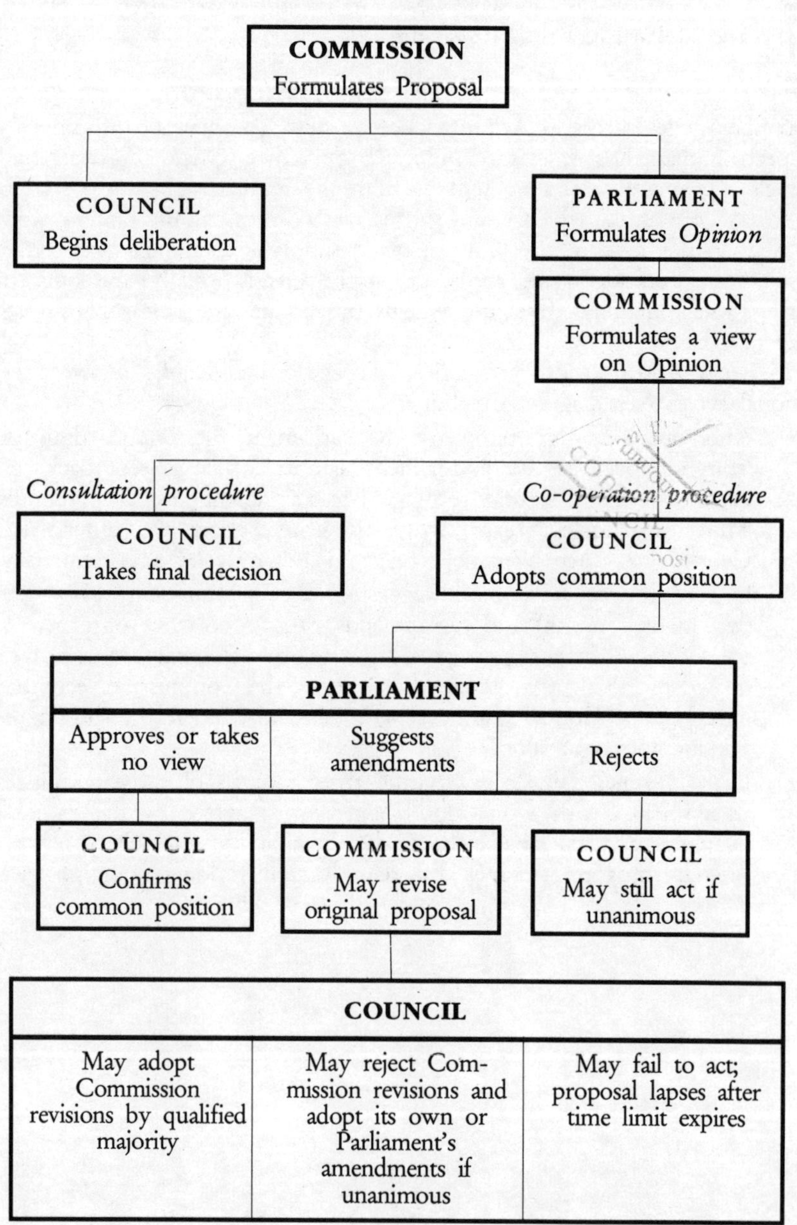

Unaccountable committees

The Treaty of Rome failed to provide for a number of matters that were bound to arise as the Community gradually dismantled its internal border controls: for example immigration by citizens of non-EC states ('third country nationals') and visa policy, the treatment of asylum-seekers, extradition, control of terrorism and drug trafficking, and police co-operation generally.[8] Article 13 of the Single European Act inserted into the Treaty a new Article 8a which flatly states: 'The internal market shall comprise an area without internal frontiers...' The *legal basis* for actually abolishing border controls, however, remains in dispute, the Act containing only a general declaration:

> In order to promote the free movement of persons, the member states shall co-operate, without prejudice to the powers of the Community, in particular as regards the entry, movement and residence of nationals of third countries. They shall also co-operate in the combating of terrorism, crime, the traffic in drugs and illicit trading in works of art and antiques.

Thus the ends are stated, but the means of achieving them are left to member states. For this reason (and perhaps others, as will become clear) the whole matter of border controls has been held to lie outside Community 'competence', and has been largely discussed by unelected inter-governmental committees which are not bound by Community rules. Such rules would have ensured that there was at least some consultation with the European Parliament, together with the publication of major decisions. As things stand, the relevant committees meet in secret and are not obliged to consult with any other Community body. The committees only rarely issue documents for public perusal.

The Parliament has naturally expressed its frustration at being thus excluded, but is powerless to change the situation; the only remedy would appear to be a revision of the Treaty of Rome, which all member states would have to ratify. The suspicion persists that the current situation well suits the more powerful governments involved (particularly the British, which objects to giving the European Parliament any real power). Even worse, national parliaments are equally kept in the dark; only occasionally is there a report to one of the European Council meetings, after which individual national parliaments may have an opportunity to discuss it and question members of their governments.

The main fora dealing with border concerns are listed below. All of them meet in secret, behind closed doors, and make decisions in the manner described above. In each case the individual EC states are represented by appropriate ministers. The Commission (but not the European Parliament) has a place by invitation in several of the groups. Their decisions are widely expected to be influenced by the Schengen Agreement and Convention (see Chapter Two) between five EC states (Belgium, France, West Germany, Luxembourg and the Netherlands); this has set precedents which many consider to be undesirable, particularly from the point of view of refugees and immigrants.

- The *Trevi Group* (named after a fountain in Rome) is led by the ministers responsible for police and security (in Britain's casc thc Home Secretary); the Commission is not represented. It was set up following a 1975 summit meeting to develop concerted action against terrorism, but now covers other forms of international crime. It has a semi-permanent secretariat and its discussions involve representatives of EC police forces. A Trevi sub-group deals specifically with the ramifications of 1992.
- The *Ad Hoc Working Group on Immigration* (hereinafter called simply the Working Group on Immigration) answers to the ministers concerned with immigration (Britain's Home Secretary again); the Commission has membership of this group.
- The *Pompidou Group*, which embraces 20 European nations (and plans to expand still further), deals specifically with drug trafficking. The Commission is now a full participant, having formerly had only observer status.
- The *Mutual Assistance Group* involves Customs and Excise officials, and has a 1992 sub-group (MAG-92). The Commission co-chairs these groups.
- The *Co-ordinators' Group* was set up following the December 1988 Rhodes summit, and includes a member of the Commission. In the definitive 'Palma Document', submitted to the 1989 Madrid summit and later reported to the British Parliament, the Co-ordinators' Group outlined all the areas of co-operation relating to the free movement of persons and defined which inter-governmental discussion groups were involved.[9]

There is a further group called European Political Co-operation, an organisation whose status was formalised by Article 30 of the Single European Act; it discusses Community foreign policy regarding non-EC states, and involves the ministers responsible for foreign affairs. In this group the European Commission plays a full role. Article 30 states that the European Parliament should be informed of issues under consideration and its views 'duly taken into consideration'.

The democratic deficit

There has been much debate within the Community on a problem which is commonly referred to as the 'democratic deficit'. The term was originally coined to cover the many complaints which members of the European Parliament make about the present system of reaching decisions affecting the Community, even where the rules of the Treaty of Rome apply:

- The Council – the chief legislature – is not a directly-elected body, but is composed of members of the executive (i.e. cabinet ministers) of each member state.
- The Commission is the main executive body of the Community but its president is not elected.
- Meetings of the Council (and especially the European Council involving heads of government) are held in secret, so the deals and alliances made are not revealed unless 'leaks' occur.
- Majority voting, extended by the Single European Act, means that ministers cannot be held accountable to their national parliaments for unwelcome Council decisions.
- Important areas of legislation – including the free movement of people and the rights of employees – are still not subject to the full co-operation procedure involving the European Parliament and the Commission (see above); even where they are, the Council has the dominant role. Matters relating to border controls are, as we have seen, outside even the Council's competence and are dealt with by unaccountable inter-government committees.
- In addition to the delegated powers given to the Committee of Permanent Representatives (see above), working groups of national civil servants advising members of the Council (a system called 'comitology') can obstruct the work of the Commission; while answerable to their own ministers, they are not accountable to the European Parliament.
- There are sectors of the EC budget over which the Parliament has only limited powers.[10]

British MPs also complain of a lack of democratic accountability, but have tended to concentrate on their inability to monitor, let alone influence, the decisions taken at Community level.[11] We discuss possible solutions below, together with the linked question of political union and its implications.

Proposals for political union

Proposals for developing closer political ties between member states have been discussed ever since the inception of the Community, this being one of the long-term aims of the Treaty of Rome: its signatories declared at the time that they were 'determined to lay the foundations of an ever closer union among the peoples of Europe'. The idea gained formal support when in 1984 the

European Parliament adopted a draft treaty for a European Union to replace the EC.[12]

The institutions of the Union were to be closely modelled on those of the EC, but with important differences in the system of accountability. Its scope for action was to be extended, with the Commission empowered to represent the Union in non-member states and international organisations, and in negotiating international agreements. Individual citizens of member states would automatically acquire citizenship of the Union, and the European Parliament elected by them would have much greater powers than before. The basic framework would thus more closely resemble that of a federal state, although the Council would continue to represent the special interests of member states.

These radical proposals did not excite much interest outside the Parliament until 1990, when political union suddenly rose to the top of the agenda for a number of reasons: the largely unspoken desire to contain a unified Germany in a stronger union with other member states; the realisation that Europe might for the first time be able to speak with one voice in dealing with the rest of the world; and, not least, the strong pressure to move towards full economic and monetary union.

Throughout this period, the Parliament persisted with efforts to obtain for itself a more meaningful role as the only assembly directly elected by the people of Europe as a whole. In 1988 a resolution was passed drawing attention to the democratic deficit,[13] and in 1990 the Parliament adopted a set of proposals (the Martin Report) for moving faster towards full union and reforming the whole system of accountability.[14] The proposals included the following new rights for the European Parliament:

- 'co-decision' with the Council for deciding Community legislation (i.e. both bodies would have to agree);
- the right to initiate legislative proposals;
- the right to give (or withhold) assent to the appointment of the Commission, the Court of Justice and the Court of Auditors;
- the right of inquiry (i.e. to call Commission officials and others before it);
- ratification of all constitutional decisions requiring ratification by member states; and
- a final say in the ratification of important international agreements and conventions entered into by the Community.

For good measure the report also recommended an extension of majority voting in the Council, more effective policies in the social and environmental fields, and incorporation of the Parliament's earlier Declaration on Fundamental Rights and Freedoms (see Chapter Six).

Sovereignty and the British Parliament

The opposition of Margaret Thatcher and her government to the whole concept of European Union (from monetary union onwards) has been presented as defending the rights of Parliament and the Crown prerogative. In view of Britain's commitment under the Treaty of Rome (see above) this position is somewhat contradictory. However, many Westminster MPs on both sides of the House have agreed with the Government, on the grounds that their authority is being increasingly bypassed by Community institutions over which they have no control. They have shown little inclination to grant more power to the European Parliament, whose members are virtually ignored by their party colleagues at Westminster.[15] Instead the aim has been to devise some way of restoring more control to Parliament in Britain.

This is perhaps where MPs and the Government part company, since the Government has not (at least until recently) shown great willingness to give Parliament enhanced opportunities to debate EC affairs. A recent report of the House of Commons Select Committee on Procedure describes the current timetabling, involving time-limited debates after 10 p.m., as 'profoundly unsatisfactory'.[16] Debates are poorly attended, partly because MPs are conscious of the futility of discussing decisions which have often already been taken. The report is particularly critical of the failure of the Government to have arranged any debate (despite numerous pleas) on matters known to have been on the agenda of the 1989 Madrid summit, where important decisions were to be taken on the first stage of economic and monetary union.[17]

In response to the report, the Government agreed to some improvements, with three new Standing Committees to consider EC documents and a twice-yearly 'forward-looking' debate of the whole House on issues likely to come up at the next summit meeting.[18] However, it remains clear that the sheer volume of EC legislation makes it inconceivable that Parliament could scrutinise everything with the same degree of attention as that expected for domestic legislation.

A further problem is that the Government has the power to decide which proposed EC legislation should be examined by the House of Commons Select Committee on European Legislation (commonly called the Scrutiny Committee). This is a curious reversal of usual democratic practice, in that the executive (the Government) decides what the directly-elected legislature (the House of Commons) can consider.

Consideration of proposed legislation by the Scrutiny Committee is in any case no guarantee that it will be debated in time by Parliament. Under a parliamentary resolution passed in 1980, ministers can decide whether for 'special reasons' they should agree to new legislation in the Council before the UK Parliament has had the opportunity to consider it.[19] In the five years between

1983 and 1988, 77 documents, designated by the Scrutiny Committee as involving questions of 'legal or political importance', were adopted by the Council prior to the completion of the scrutiny process.[20]

Quite apart from the impossibility of scrutinising all EC legislation in detail, there is a fundamental difficulty in sustaining the argument for unfettered sovereignty in the context of the Single European Act and the use of majority voting. In this respect other EC countries would appear to have a less ambivalent approach; one argument is that they are less attached to a particular, unchanging tradition of parliamentary democracy, and do not equate national identity with the sovereignty associated with their national parliaments.[21]

The British Government insists that there is no fundamental problem, saying merely: 'The basic democratic structure of the Community is that member state governments take decisions in the Council of Ministers, and are accountable to national parliaments for their actions'.[22] The House of Commons Select Committee on Procedure has, however, demolished this position without mercy:

> ...European legislation is initiated almost exclusively by an executive organisation (the Commission) with which the United Kingdom Parliament has no formal relationship and over which it has no direct control. More importantly, the United Kingdom has, as a condition of its Community membership, bound itself to accept the collective authority of a legislative body (the Council of Ministers) only one of whose 12 members is accountable to the House of Commons. These facts may be unwelcome in some quarters, but they spring unavoidably from the United Kingdom's Treaty obligations.[23]

The federalist position

At the other end of the spectrum of views on the evolution of the Community is the passionate belief (predating the creation of the EC) in the ideal of a united, federal Europe. Author Ernest Wistrich, for example, sees federalism as the most democratic solution to current dissatisfaction over the constitutional arrangements of the Community. By giving less power to national governments and at the same time more local autonomy, he also sees federalism as an answer to the intractable problems of disaffected regions within larger states: he cites moves that have already taken place in this direction in Spain, and suggests that the problems of Northern Ireland might be soluble if both Britain and the Irish Republic were to join a European political union.[24]

Wistrich sees such a federation as potentially less, not more, centralised than the present system; like those on the other side of the argument, he claims in support the concept of 'subsidiarity' – an elastic term meaning in essence that decisions are taken as close to the citizen as possible. In Wistrich's vision of a federal Europe, the institutions of the EC will stand at the summit of various levels of decision-making. His Commission will not be a collection of national nominees but a European Cabinet, chosen by a Commission President who is directly elected by the people of the United States of Europe.

At present the federal model is not supported by most Community governments, though West Germany (itself a federal democracy) is said to favour the idea, provided that greater democracy can be introduced into the workings of the EC.[25] An inter-governmental conference will convene in December 1990 to consider the issue, though early indications are that it will not move as far towards union as some (including Commission President Jacques Delors) have hoped.[26] Meanwhile, it is clear from recent press reports that opinion among a growing number of British politicians is swinging round to at least considering the idea.

Democracy as a civil liberties issue

International treaties on human rights and civil liberties have long insisted on the need for a democratic system in which citizens fully participate; democracy is held to be a source from which other civil liberties flow.

For example, the UN's Universal Declaration of Human Rights, adopted in 1948, states: 'Everyone has the right to take part in the government of his country directly or through freely chosen representatives'. Article 3 of the European Convention on Human Rights (see Chapter Six) further commits the signatories to hold 'free elections... which will ensure the free expression of the opinion of the people in the choice of the legislature'. The UN's 1976 Covenant on Civil and Political Rights also guarantees every citizen 'the right and the opportunity... to take part in the conduct of public affairs'

The failure of the EC's current structure to measure up to these standards has led some to argue that only withdrawal from the EC can restore to the British people their lost democratic rights. While perfectly tenable from a civil liberty point of view, this position is clearly not exclusively valid. A more realistic approach, given the current positions of the major political parties – and one which underlies the treatment of other issues considered in this book – is to look constructively instead at the various proposals for democratic reform.

Such proposals need to be examined in the light of the international criteria outlined above: free elections for major decision-making bodies and democratic participation in public life. If the proposals pass that basic civil liberty test, then other criteria for potential benefit to the Community such as political harmony between states, economic consequences and so on (which are beyond the scope of this book to consider) can help determine their acceptability.

The current lack of proper human rights monitoring within the Community (see above and Chapter Six) also demands attention. Incorporation of human rights legislation into Community and domestic law would form a further safeguard for basic civil liberties against any abuse arising from a reformed structure.

Finally, it is instructive to note the determination of several of the new democracies of Eastern Europe to adopt carefully designed electoral systems which ensure the adequate representation of regional and minority groups. All have abandoned, without hesitation, the 'democratic centralist' systems under which they previously laboured, where decisions were made behind closed doors by members of a ruling élite. It would be ironic in the extreme if these new democracies, anxious to enter the embrace of the European Community, were to face an unreformed system that was less democratic than their own.

Notes

1. Ernest Wistrich, *After 1992: the United States of Europe* (Routledge, 1989), pp. 23-7. For a recent summary of the Council of Europe's activities and prospects, see *Forum* 2/89 (Council of Europe, Strasbourg). For lists of members and committees, see *Vacher's European Companion & Consultants' Register* (Kerswill, Berkhamsted; published quarterly).
2. For a short history and account of the workings of Community institutions, see: Emile Noël, *Working Together: the Institutions of the European Community* (Office for Official Publications of the European Communities, Luxembourg, 1988). See also: Stanley A. Budd and Alun Jones, *The European Community: a Guide to the Maze*, 3rd Edn (Kogan Page, 1989) and Stephen Crampton, *1992 Eurospeak Explained* (Rosters, 1990).
3. Ernest Wistrich, *After 1992: the United States of Europe* (Routledge, 1989), p. 99.
4. For details of the Court's procedures, see: Neill Nugent, *The Government and Politics of the European Community* (Macmillan, 1990), pp. 142-65.
5. Phil Fennell, 'The Court of First Instance', in *European Access*, February 1990, pp. 11-12.
6. *The Independent*, 20 June 1990.
7. Emile Noël, *Working Together: the Institutions of the European Community* (Office for Official Publications of the European Communities, Luxembourg, 1988), p. 26.
8. Alan Butt Philip, *European Border Controls: Who Needs Them?* (Royal Institute of International Affairs, London, 1989), p. 23.
9. House of Lords Select Committee on the European Communities, *1992: Border Controls of People*, Session 1988-89, 22nd Report (HMSO, London, 1989), Report Appendix 5.

10. M. Toussaint (rapporteur), *Report on the Democratic Deficit in the European Community*, A2-276/87 (European Parliament, 1988).
11. House of Commons Foreign Affairs Committee, *The Operation of the Single European Act*, Session 1989-90, 2nd Report (HMSO, London, 1990), para. 53.
12. *Official Journal of the European Communities*, C77 (19 March 1984), pp. 33-54.
13. *Ibid.*, C187 (18 July 1988), p. 229.
14. David Martin (rapporteur), *Interim Report on the Intergovernmental Conference in the Context of Parliament's Strategy for European Union*, A3-47/90 (European Parliament, 1990). For the amended resolution adopting the report, see *Official Journal of the European Communities*, C96 (17 April 1990), pp. 114-18.
15. John Palmer, 'Having a real say in Europe', in *The Guardian*, 13 December 1989.
16. House of Commons Select Committee on Procedure, *The Scrutiny of European Legislation*, Session 1988-89, 4th Report (HMSO, London, 1989), para. 43.
17. *Ibid.*, paras 43 and 46.
18. *The Scrutiny of European Legislation: Government Response,* Cm. 1081 (HMSO, London, 1990).
19. House of Commons Select Committee on Procedure, *The Scrutiny of European Legislation*, Session 1988-89, 4th Report (HMSO, London, 1989), para. 8.
20. *Ibid.*, para. 15.
21. House of Commons Foreign Affairs Committee, *The Operation of the Single European Act*, Session 1989-90, 2nd Report (HMSO, London, 1990), para. 34.
22. *The Operation of the Single European Act: Observations by the Government*, Cm. 1077 (HMSO, 1990), para. 19.
23. House of Commons Select Committee on Procedure, *The Scrutiny of European Legislation*, Session 1988-89, 4th Report (HMSO, London, 1989), para. 10.
24. Ernest Wistrich, *After 1992: the United States of Europe* (Routledge, 1989), pp. 138-40. See also: Christopher Layton, *The Healing of Europe* (Federal Trust, London, 1990).
25. John Palmer, 'Z-bends on the road to a United States of Europe', in *The Guardian*, 18 May 1990.
26. *The Guardian*, 21 May 1990.

CHAPTER TWO

Fortress Europe

While attractive as a distant prospect, the European Community's long-standing aim of abolishing internal frontiers set off loud alarm bells in every country as soon as it looked like becoming a reality. Businessmen, wishing to do away with tiresome tariffs and delays at borders, saw only a rosy vista of expanding markets. Politicians, however, some of whom have relied for electoral support on a policy of tight immigration controls and discrimination against non-citizens, saw it rather differently. Other vested interests were unhappy, not least customs officials whose jobs seemed likely to evaporate. The British Government, in particular, suddenly discovered objections to a number of features of the Single European Act (see Introduction) which in 1986 it had pushed through a doubtful Parliament on a three-line whip.

In response to these worries, EC governments set about reassuring the people of the Community that everything would be all right provided that what they defined as 'problems' – a term generally stretched to include immigrants and refugees as well as terrorism, international crime and drug trafficking – were rigidly excluded from the external borders of the Community.

The concept of a 'ring fence' surrounding what has been dubbed 'Fortress Europe' rapidly came to dominate the planning of EC governments. The liberal commitment to free movement of people within the Community has been counterbalanced by the idea of concentrating and intensifying at external borders all the checks that formerly took place at each frontier. In case this proved insufficient to prevent a 'problem' from leaking in, it was agreed that random internal checks away from borders would also have to be multiplied.[1] For some people all this begins to look like less, rather than more, freedom.

Behind closed doors

We have seen in Chapter One that the Treaty of Rome, even as amended by the Single European Act, fails to give the institutions of the Community clear authority to deal with such matters as immigration from outside the EC, visa policy, asylum for refugees, extradition and cross-border co-operation between police forces.[2] As a result, all these vital and sensitive issues are discussed in committees like the Trevi Group and the Working Group on Immigration, which operate outside the Community's system of consultation and accountability (such as it is).

The consequences of this omission are illustrated most graphically by the text of the Palma Document drawn up by the Co-ordinators' Group (see

Chapter One).[3] This followed a Commission report on the abolition of border controls for people.[4] The Palma Document shows just how many of the issues are being discussed and settled by non-EC groups. It includes a detailed list of topics together with measures considered 'essential' or 'desirable', and the proposed timetable for their implementation before the end of 1992 (see Appendix I for the more relevant items). The required measures for harmonisation are summarised under two main headings of visa policy and asylum policy. The first heading covers the following:

- establishment of a common list of countries whose citizens are subject to a visa requirement;
- establishment of a common list of persons to be refused entry;
- harmonisation of the criteria for granting visas, while allowing the specific circumstances of certain applicants to be taken into account;
- a European visa.

Under 'grant of asylum and refugee status' the document says that policy will initially focus on the following aspects:

- acceptance of identical international commitments with regard to asylum;
- determining the state responsible for examining the application for asylum;
- simplified or priority procedure for the examination of clearly unfounded requests;
- conditions governing the movement of the applicant between member states;
- study of the need for a financing system to fund the economic consequences of implementing the common policy.

Probably few people are aware of the extent of the changes proposed in the Palma Document, or that many of these changes have either already been agreed or will shortly be settled behind closed doors. Recent events in Eastern Europe may lead to the postponement of some decisions, but the principles have already been laid down. Many of the proposals have implications which have thoroughly alarmed some of the data protection authorities in the EC (see Chapter Three). The oblique phrases used to describe some of the measures (particularly those relating to refugees) are reminiscent of the 'newspeak' in Orwell's *Nineteen Eighty-Four*, and have raised instant suspicion among refugee and immigrant groups.

The document does contain a warning of the dangers: 'In keeping with the traditional values of the member states of the Community, the Co-ordinators insist that the stepping-up of controls at external frontiers should not go beyond what is strictly necessary for safeguarding security and law and order in the member states.' It also draws attention to the Declaration against Racism and Xenophobia adopted in 1986 by the European Parliament, the Council, representatives of the member states and the Commission (see Appendix II). Apart from the question of what Europe's 'traditional values' really are where racism and xenophobia are concerned, the unfortunate reality is that the Co-ordinators are appointed representatives with no control over the actions of their governments. If their warnings were to be taken seriously it would be harder for governments such as Britain's to persist in classifying apparently genuine refugees as 'economic migrants', and to pursue policies that hinder the reunion of families in so many ways.

The Schengen precedent

In 1985 five countries – France, West Germany and the Benelux countries (Belgium, Luxembourg and the Netherlands) – signed a formal agreement at Schengen in Luxembourg to abolish their internal border controls ahead of the rest of the EC.[5] A further, more detailed Convention was to be signed in June 1989, but because of various disagreements this was postponed until the end of that year; by then the momentous changes in Eastern Europe were under way, and the negotiations stalled again because of West German insistence that East German citizens should be given formal rights under the agreement.

This question was resolved following the rapid progress made towards unification of the two Germanies, but the French Government remained unhappy over data protection aspects of the agreement. Negotiations resumed in April 1990, and a detailed *Convention of Application of the Schengen Agreement* (called in this book the Schengen Convention) was signed in June 1990. It will come into force only after ratification by all Schengen member states, which means by mid-1991 at the earliest.

The provisions of the Schengen Convention are an example – and in many ways a warning – of the way in which internal controls and border policies are likely to develop throughout the Community. Certainly it would be hard for the precedent set by the Convention to be ignored, since only three land borders in the Community (Denmark-Germany, UK-Republic of Ireland and Spain-Portugal) do not involve one of its signatories. Italy has already said it wants to join as soon as possible, and Spain and Portugal have also signalled interest.[6]

The Schengen Convention covers the same ground as the Palma Document: the abolition of border controls and the harmonisation of policies on immigration, drugs, firearms, and so on. It also deals with police co-operation, including 'hot pursuit' operations across borders. The detailed provisions include the following features:

- There will be increased policing of external borders and detailed checks on those entering from outside the Schengen area: these checks will cover (as a minimum) establishing personal identity following the presentation of travel documents. Persons and vehicles may be searched in accordance with national laws.
- Citizens of non-EC countries will be subject to particularly stringent checks, not only on entering but also on leaving. On arrival they may be required to present not just visas but documents justifying the purpose of the visit, and may need to demonstrate adequate means of subsistence. Admission will normally be limited to a period of three months, during which freedom of movement is allowed between member states of the Convention unless entry into the Schengen area is subject to a visa carrying limitations. This freedom of movement will not extend to those admitted for longer periods by one of the Schengen countries. There will be a common list of 'undesirable aliens' – non-EC citizens to be refused entry. After entering, non-EC citizens must register with the authorities of the country in which they are staying, and again if they move to another Schengen state. They can also be expelled from the Schengen area if they are deemed to constitute a threat to 'public order, national security or international relations'.
- A uniform Schengen visa valid for only three months will be introduced, but meanwhile an equivalent visa issued by one Schengen state will be valid in others unless it carries territorial limitations. Such 'harmonisation' implies that a common list will be drawn up of countries whose nationals will require visas. The list is widely expected to cover virtually all Third World countries (i.e. those with non-white populations). In secret negotiations between all the EC states, the Trevi Group and the Working Group on Immigration are also drawing up such a common list. In both cases the number of countries on it is likely to be at least 60, and in the case of the Schengen group it is said to be 115.[5]
- All member countries will introduce legislation under which any shipping company or airline bringing in a non-EC national without valid documents will be penalised (as in Britain's carrier liability legislation, discussed below). The carrier may be required to take the person back to another country, and this will also apply to those refused entry at land borders of the Schengen area.
- A 'one chance only' rule will apply to asylum-seekers. Only one Schengen country will handle a given application, on the basis of complex rules as to which country should be responsible; an asylum-seeker refused entry cannot then go to a second Schengen

signatory. Among EC states, a very similar arrangement has been incorporated into a new inter-governmental Convention (see below).

- Each Schengen state guarantees to ensure that everyone (including all EC nationals) who stays in a hotel or lodging house, and even on a camping site or on a hired boat, must fill in a form and show proof of identity; such forms are to be stored or passed on to those authorised to use them in searches for missing or wanted persons.
- Cross-border surveillance and 'hot pursuit' by uniformed police (including powers of apprehension until local police take over) are allowed, subject to different limitations set by each country concerned. Firearms may be used in self-defence.
- A computerised Schengen Information System (SIS) is being set up to store information on wanted or missing persons, vehicles and other items stolen or missing, non-EC nationals to be refused admission at borders, persons to be extradited or expelled, and persons or vehicles under covert surveillance. In the last case the details of (say) a car, its occupants and the route followed can be recorded; the system is intended for use not only at external borders but within countries as well, presumably by using mobile computer terminals. Agencies dealing with applications for visas and residence permits, and with the movements of non-EC citizens within the Schengen area, will have access to the system. One apparent change, however, made since earlier proposals were leaked,[5] is that details of asylum requests are not included in the list of data that may be recorded on the SIS; in this case the exchange of information is subject to separate rules (see below).

The European Commission had observer status at the Schengen meetings and expressed no disagreement with the terms of the 1985 agreement; indeed, the Commission was later strongly in favour of negotiations getting under way again as soon as possible. The Schengen Convention provides for any member state of the EC to join, and allows for the fact that after 1992 the Convention may have to be modified in the light of EC agreements on abolishing border controls. However, it seems much more likely that Schengen will form the model for the EC. This has both positive and negative aspects, as we discuss below.

Schengen and the Geneva Convention on refugees

The discussions leading up to the Schengen Convention were held in secret, and (as in the case of discussion groups like Trevi) the proceedings did not involve consultation with European or national parliaments. Important issues only emerged when negotiations stalled because of disagreement between the parties, as for instance when the French negotiators became unhappy at the data protection implications of the SIS (see below and Chapter Three). Most disturbing of all, the United Nations High Commission for Refugees (UNHCR) – a body set up by the international community to deal with some of the very problems under discussion – was not admitted to the Schengen meetings.

Although details of the discussions emerged only as unofficial leaks, intense lobbying by non-governmental organisations did lead national parliaments (particularly in the Netherlands) to demand a public debate on the issues being discussed, and the European Parliament passed a highly critical resolution on the subject.[7] Among other things, the resolution made the following points:

- The Geneva Convention on refugees and its 1967 Protocol, ratified by all EC states, provides for co-operation with the UNHCR on matters relating to refugees.
- The 1944 Chicago Convention on International Aviation prohibits fines on airlines transporting passengers with inadequate documents.
- There are grounds for arguing that the European Commission does, in fact, have competence to make proposals relating to asylum, and the Parliament believes that the Commission should intervene under Article 169 of the Treaty of Rome (which gives it this right when a member state of the EC has failed to fulfil its obligations under the Treaty).

The resolution also roundly condemned the way in which the governments of EC states use the Trevi Group and Working Group on Immigration, calling it a violation of international conventions and democratic principles.

As a belated recognition of this concern, and again at Dutch insistence, the Schengen Convention contains a declaration that nothing in it should conflict with the obligations of states under the Geneva Convention (see below). There is also a promise to co-operate with UNHCR on matters relating to refugees. The problem is, as the Schengen signatories must have known, that while it is possible to argue that the Schengen Convention breaches the *spirit* of the Geneva Convention, the latter Convention does not specifically outlaw such measures as carrier liability legislation; these measures make it much harder for refugees to even reach the border in order to seek asylum.[8] We return to this point below in connection with the EC as a whole.

Data protection and the Schengen Convention

Data protection is the one area where the Schengen precedent could actually be of long-term benefit to civil liberties in the larger Community. The Schengen Convention lays down rules concerning how much information may be exchanged between states when a refugee seeks asylum, for the purpose of establishing which state is responsible for examining the request. The information is limited to certain categories:

- personal data such as name, place and date of birth and nationality;
- identity and travel documents, or other information to establish identity;
- places stayed at and route followed;
- any visas or residence permits issued by a Schengen state;
- placc where asylum was claimed; and
- details of any previous claim, or state of progress of a current claim.

The sensitive nature of such information is clear: if it found its way back to the refugee's country of origin, it might harm the person's family or associates and make it even harder for others to follow the same route. Given that the whole system is likely to make life harder for asylum seekers, the Schengen Convention does at least include strict rules for exchanging data on them. Firstly, an asylum seeker will have the right to see the relevant information and have it corrected or erased. Secondly, there are limits on retaining the data; and most importantly, data recorded in a Schengen country can only be computerised if the country concerned has adopted legislation conforming to the Council of Europe Convention on data protection (see Chapter Three). In the latter case there must also be an independent national data protection authority to monitor compliance. If the data are not computerised, the authority is still supposed to ensure adequate protection.

As regards the Schengen Information System, similar rules apply and there is an absolute ban on the transmission of data between two countries unless both of them have appropriate data protection legislation in force. This was aimed initially at Belgium, where a Bill on data protection was only introduced in January 1990, but it would also apply to any new member. In any case, the data files of one country will not be open to access by another – each country regulates what is transmitted to others.

In some respects the Schengen rules on data protection are well in advance of those applying in many other countries, including the UK. The Schengen Convention requires that 'sensitive data' as defined in the Council of Europe Convention (data on racial origin, political opinions, religious or other beliefs, health or sexual life) must not be incorporated in the system; furthermore, specific mention is made of the Council of Europe Recommendation R (87) 15 concerning data held by the police (see Chapter Three). In addition, in each country the agency managing the system is to monitor (on average) every tenth transmission of personal data, to check that the rules are not being broken.

As an overall safeguard, there is to be a technical support organisation (based in Strasbourg and managed by France) to perform a number of functions, including notification of time limits for erasing various categories of data. This will be run by a joint authority comprising representatives from each country, which will also look into difficulties that arise when the system is in use.

The meticulous rules laid down for data protection (not all of which have been described here) should form a useful model for comparable information exchange systems in the wider European Community, and national data protection authorities will have a yardstick for their own data protection laws We return to this general topic in Chapter Three.

The British position on border controls

While the signatories of the Schengen Convention are moving ahead with the complete abolition of internal border controls, and other EC states seem largely ready to follow suit by the end of 1992, the British Government does not accept that significant changes in its border control system need to take place at all. The Government disagreed strongly with the statement in the Commission's 1988 paper on the abolition of internal border controls that 'anyone with intimate knowledge of these matters knows that the present frontier controls are ineffective'.[4] Douglas Hurd, when Home Secretary, said to the House of Commons: 'The Commission's report misunderstands the value of these important frontier checks',[9] while Mrs Thatcher told a newspaper reporter: 'I did not join Europe to have free movement of terrorists, criminals, drugs, plant and animal diseases and rabies, and illegal immigrants.'[10]

In support of this view the Government quotes the General Declaration appended (at British insistence) to the Single European Act:

> Nothing in these provisions shall affect the right of the member states to take such measures as they consider necessary for the purpose of controlling immigration from third countries, and to combat terrorism, the traffic in drugs and illicit trading in works of art and antiques.

The Government's position has not changed since the issue of a Home Office memorandum in 1989:

> ...the way forward is to combine measures to strengthen the external frontier of the Community, and other forms of co-operation between states, with such measures as are required at the national frontier to control the immigration of non-Community nationals into the United Kingdom.[11]

The Government insists that this does not mean the abolition of passport checks on travellers from Europe, claiming that Britain's position as an island nation is different because its 'internal' (Community) borders coincide with its external borders with the rest of the world. There will be (as at present) a 'streamlined channel' for EC nationals in which most travellers do no more than display the outer covers of their passports, together with more detailed spot checks on individuals. Mr Hurd claimed in 1989 that the mere provision of an EC passport channel was 'a practical indication of our commitment to the Single European Act',[12] but it remains to be seen whether this is accepted as sufficient by the Commission and the rest of the Community (see also Chapter Four).

The Scandinavian dilemma

To confuse the border control issue still further, Denmark is in the anomalous position of already being a member of the Nordic Union of Scandinavian countries (with Finland, Iceland, Norway and Sweden) which has an agreement for free travel between them; no passport is needed, and a driving licence is sufficient when crossing borders. Since only Denmark out of these is an EC member, the question arises as to how the 'external border' of the EC is to be defined. The Commission takes the view that this is a problem for Denmark to sort out. Article 234 of the Treaty of Rome lays down that existing agreements between a member state and a non-EC state are not affected by the Treaty; however, it then demands that where such an agreement is incompatible with the Treaty the member state shall 'take all appropriate steps to eliminate the incompatibilities established'. The problem remains at present unresolved.

Refugees – a betrayal of trust?

The way in which border control issues are eventually resolved within the EC will inevitably have a significant impact on refugees. The number of refugees seeking asylum in Europe has risen dramatically in recent years, from 70,500 in 1983 to 237,400 in 1988; of these only 3,300 applied to Britain. The British Government has, however, been in the forefront of action taken by many countries to restrict their entry. According to UN estimates, in 1987 Belgium granted refugee status to 2,683 people, France 8,635, West Germany 8,231 but Britain only 536[13] – 16 per cent of those who applied, compared with 83 per cent in 1980.[14]

The UN's 1948 Universal Declaration of Human Rights, which the 1988 Rhodes summit meeting of EC heads of government promised to uphold, lays down that 'everyone has the right to seek and enjoy in other countries asylum from persecution'.[8] The 1951 Convention Relating to the Status of Refugees (the Geneva Convention), also a UN treaty to which all EC countries subscribe, is silent on the right to asylum.[15] However, it assumes that a refugee has by definition left his or her country of origin. Working on the same assumption, Article 31 lays down that refugees shall not be penalised for arriving in another country unlawfully if their lives or freedom are at risk; they must then be allowed either to apply for refugee status or seek admission to another country. Article 32 forbids arbitrary expulsion without a proper appeal procedure, and again requires that an opportunity be given to seek admission elsewhere. Article 33 prohibits 'refoulement' – sending refugees back to any country where their lives or freedom would be threatened on account of their 'race, religion, nationality, membership of a particular social group or political opinion'.

Britain and an increasing number of other European countries have taken two steps to restrict the arrival of refugees, which, though passed into law, are widely believed to be in breach of the Geneva Convention. Firstly, a requirement has been imposed on all individuals from 'refugee-producing' countries that visas must be obtained before travelling. Secondly, airlines and other carriers have been made liable to incur penalties for allowing people to travel without such visas; in Britain the Immigration (Carriers' Liability) Act 1987 imposes a fine of £1,000 for each person accepted without proper documents. The combined effects of this Act and the visa rules were heavily criticised by a High Court judge in 1990 when he overturned a Home Office decision to refuse to consider some asylum applications.[16] We have seen above, however, that such practices are now an integral part of the Schengen Convention between five other EC states.

The difficulty all this presents to a potential refugee is clear: it may be dangerous to be seen visiting a foreign consulate to request a visa (particularly if the person is normally in hiding), and British consulates have in any case no general power to grant refugee status. As the judge pointed out in the case referred to above, intending refugees cannot anyway obtain visas on the basis of being refugees in the countries where they are being persecuted, because at that stage they are not outside their country of nationality and do not fall within the accepted definition of a refugee.[16] The wait for a visa may be extremely long (as potential immigrants to Britain from the Indian sub-continent know to their cost), and it may never be granted.

As if this legal barrier were not enough, countries operating such policies have increasingly sent refugees back to their country of origin in apparent breach of the Geneva Convention. In Britain there is now supposed to be a procedure whereby a person claiming asylum and rejected by immigration officials is referred for help and advice to a Refugee Unit associated with the United Kingdom Immigrants Advisory Service (UKIAS). However, this has not prevented blatant abuses such as that which occurred in June 1989 when Kurdish refugees were detained on entry and forced on to planes back to Turkey. The Home Office later admitted that immigration officials broke the law and agreed to pay compensation, including damages for distress and assault.[17] Generally, government ministers insist that the majority of asylum applicants are no more than 'economic migrants' seeking a higher standard of living, despite frequent evidence to the contrary.

One may ask how this situation can arise when a country like Britain subscribes not only to the Geneva Convention but also to the 1967 Protocol, which gives a supervisory role to the United Nations High Commissioner for Refugees. In evidence given to the House of Lords in 1989, the Commissioner's representative made it clear that, in her view, carrier liability legislation was 'contrary to the spirit and intent and purpose of the Convention', and that the Commissioner was concerned about the effect of visa requirements in limiting access to asylum.[13] However, when asked about the Commissioner's powers of sanction if either one country or the whole of Europe went against the Convention, she replied 'I am afraid we do not have any'.[13]

When one adds to this the fact that the Geneva Convention contains no right of individual petition to an international court over cases of abuse, it is clear that any country – or the EC as a whole – can simply ignore the Convention or misinterpret it. The only method of appeal against such abuses is the lengthy procedure of taking a case to the European Court of Human Rights, citing general principles such as that embodied in Article 3 of the European Convention on Human Rights, which says: 'No one shall be subjected to torture or to inhuman or degrading treatment or punishment'.[18]

EC policy on refugees

In 1985 the European Commission announced that, by 1988 at the latest, it would make a proposal for a Directive on the harmonisation of asylum law and the situation of refugees. No text, however, was published, though leaked details emerged at the end of 1988.[8] There appear to have been objections from some member states, particularly those who were negotiating a somewhat harsher set of rules for the draft Schengen Convention. Some took the view that the Commission had no competence to deal with the matter. The Commission has now retreated to the position that it is concerned not with the general principles underlying the grant of asylum, but only with harmonising EC practice. Instead of persisting with a Directive, the Commission encouraged the adoption of an inter-government Convention for which it would not be directly responsible (see below).

In May 1988 the ministers of the Working Group on Immigration adopted an agreement designed to prevent people from seeking asylum in more than one country.[19] In December 1989 the same Working Group announced its intention of concluding two inter-government Conventions during 1990, one on the crossing of external EC borders and the other on the designation of the state responsible for examining an application for asylum.[20]

There was, as in the case of the Schengen Convention (see above), some wrangling between governments over the details of the asylum Convention; each government was keen to expedite the examination of asylum requests, while ensuring that the rules divert as many refugees as possible to some other member state. In the event, a new 'Convention determining the state responsible for examining applications for asylum lodged in one of the member states of the European Community' emerged at almost the same time as the signing of the Schengen Convention in June 1990.

The new Convention (called in this book the European Asylum Convention) is very similar in content to the relevant part of the Schengen Convention, and its provisions for data protection are identical; information on requests can only be exchanged between states where both of them have appropriate legislation in force and an independent data protection authority. Manual as well as computerised data are covered, and the asylum seeker has a right of access to the data. The rules are not, however, as stringent as those governing the Schengen Information System (see above).

Complex conditions are laid down for determining which state is responsible for examining an asylum request; the guiding principle is that any state which has issued a visa or residence permit is the responsible state, with rules to decide cases where the refugee has more than one such document. If a refugee crossed the external borders of the EC illegally, the state whose border was crossed is responsible – unless the refugee managed to stay undetected in another state for at least six months.

All this is clearly designed to encourage member states to be zealous in guarding their frontiers and hunting down illegal entrants; it may well also discourage the granting of visas to people who seem likely to claim asylum, because they are then likely to become the sole responsibility of the state granting the visa. The new Convention anticipates that in due course there will be a common visa list for the EC and a 'harmonised' asylum policy, in which case the Convention will be revised.

The only obvious advantage of the Convention over the previous arrangement is that, although an asylum-seeker has only one chance of being accepted by an EC state, the request must at least be considered by one of these states; at present this is not the case. As in the case of Schengen, the signatories of the European Asylum Convention assert the primacy of the Geneva Convention on refugees and its 1967 Protocol, and express their intention of 'pursuing dialogue' with the UN High Commission for Refugees (UNHCR). The latter body was not party to the discussions, but was consulted over the drafting, and some (though apparently not all) of its suggestions were incorporated. The final attitude of UNHCR to the European Asylum Convention will no doubt depend on how it is seen to work in practice.

The view of the European Commission (which incidentally is charged with providing a secretariat to service the Convention) has been that, whatever misgivings observers might have about the content of the European Asylum

Convention, it is not intended to conflict with the Geneva Convention and will in any case have to be ratified by national parliaments because it is an international treaty. So far as the UK is concerned, however, the Convention will merely be 'laid before Parliament' for three weeks before the Government ratifies it; Parliament will be able to debate it but not prevent ratification. (This is because no change in domestic legislation is required; the Government uses the Crown prerogative under the so-called 'Ponsonby rule'.)

The European Parliament has long been concerned about the situation facing refugees. In 1987 it adopted a report on the right to asylum (the Vetter Report)[21] which contained extensive recommendations on the better treatment of refugees; it criticised the use of visa restrictions and other deterrent measures, and proposed that refugees accepted by an EC state should have the same rights as EC nationals. As in other areas, the Parliament gave greater weight to human rights than did the secret conclaves of ministers from member states, but its proposals have fallen on deaf ears.

The outlook for refugees would therefore appear bleak. Harmonisation of asylum procedures will not be accompanied by freedom of movement between EC states for those admitted as refugees. The Schengen Convention requires that carrier liability be extended to all its member countries, and there seems little doubt that its adoption will spread; Britain already has such legislation (see above). The European Commission takes no position on the issue. In addition, both Schengen and EC groups have been drawing up increasingly long lists of countries from which visas will be required. It is highly unlikely that countries with policies more liberal than the norm will be allowed to continue with them; a 'lowest common standard' will apply.

It is not surprising, therefore, that extreme dismay has been expressed by all the groups working on behalf of refugees. At European level, the umbrella organisation European Consultation on Refugees and Exiles (ECRE) has deplored the lack of political will to address the real needs of refugees.[22] In Britain the Refugee Council,[23] the Joint Council for the Welfare of Immigrants (JCWI),[24] Amnesty International[25], the Runnymede Trust[19] and even the government-sponsored United Kingdom Immigrants Advisory Service (UKIAS) have deplored the current trends in refugee policy.[26] Many grass-roots refugee groups such as those which compose the Refugee Forum (an association of refugee self-help groups) have expressed anger at the way the situation seems set to become even worse than it already is, not only for refugees but for all black residents of Europe.[27] Such groups also mistrust the government-funded refugee assistance bodies that seem unable to influence the situation.

The underlying problem is that Europe is unprepared to face the realities of the world-wide refugee situation. Only five per cent of the world's refugees seek asylum in Western Europe, and the refugee population is very small compared with that elsewhere. Britain has a refugee population of about 140,000 or one for every 400 people in the country, compared with one in four in Jordan and one in 25 in Sudan.[19] Refugees are regarded as an unfortunate Third World problem for which European nations bear no responsibility. Yet many of the refugees have fled because of conflicts instigated or fuelled by superpower rivalries, in which European governments and companies have enthusiastically sold arms to the combatants. It is also strongly argued by some that the EC's external trading policies after 1992 will deepen the economic depression of much of the Third World;[28] this will inevitably contribute to political instability and the generation of even more refugees. The European Community has an opportunity – at present being overlooked in its obsession with the internal market and external border controls – to look beyond its borders and address the underlying causes of the international refugee crisis.[29]

Unequal rights for immigrants

If the prospect for refugees appears bad, that facing other potential immigrants and those already living in the EC is little better. Article 48 of the Treaty of Rome demands freedom of movement and no discrimination based on nationality for 'workers of the member states', without specifying that they should also be *nationals* (i.e. full citizens) of such states, and some have argued that the founders of the Community did not intend such a restriction. However, EC law and policy have developed on the assumption that the Treaty refers here to nationals of member states, and in practice EC nationals have greatly superior rights to non-EC ('third country') nationals living and working in the Community.

The term 'migrant' refers in Eurospeak only to EC nationals who migrate to other EC countries. However, many millions of non-EC nationals live in the Community: more than 10 million according to a recent account,[30] and certainly not less than eight million, the number 'documented or in a regular situation residing and working' (i.e. legally working) in an EC state.[31] Nearly one million of the latter are recorded for the UK.

The UK's total will include a small but unknown proportion who have British-issued passports but not full citizenship under the complex rules laid down in the 1981 British Nationality Act;[32] of these, only Gibraltarians were exceptionally included by the British Government as UK citizens for the purposes of EC law. Most of the others are black citizens of Commonwealth countries who have long been settled in the UK. As things stand, 1992 will exclude all such people from the benefits of freedom of movement. It will also strengthen the measures that already exclude many who wish to enter from outside as visitors, students, workers or relatives of non-EC nationals living here.

Increased visa requirements and steps to prevent unwanted immigration will ensure this.

Rights of EC nationals and dependants

The Treaty of Rome gave nationals of member states the right to cross internal borders for purposes of employment, self-employment or for the provision of services. Similar rights apply to a migrant's spouse, children and certain relatives; such people may require visas if they are not EC nationals, but this cannot be refused if the marriage relationship is recognised by law.[33]

In the context of 1992 the Commission has recently made a number of new proposals. Firstly, it has drawn up three draft Directives to extend freedom of movement and the right of residence to other categories of EC national such as students, pensioners and others who are self-supporting but not 'economically active'. Secondly, the Commission has proposed minor changes to strengthen entitlement to residence permits and to give greater security to migrant workers and their dependants during periods of unemployment; there will also be protection for a spouse and dependants in the event of the death of the worker or dissolution of the marriage.[34]

Thirdly (and most controversially) the Commission has proposed extending the categories of family members entitled to join EC nationals who work in another EC state: included now would be 'any other member of the family dependent on or living under the roof of the worker or spouse in the country from whence they came'.[35]

This last aroused familiar objections from the political right when the issue was debated in the British Parliament, on the grounds that it would unleash a flood of unwanted immigrants into Britain. A more pertinent point was made by Alistair Darling MP, who observed that the proposed changes would compound the current situation under which greater rights of family unity are available to EC citizens coming to Britain than to British citizens already living here:

> At present, a Frenchman can marry a woman from Pakistan, for example, and can enter the United Kingdom if he is a worker within the meaning of European legislation. He could also be joined by his children under 21 and by his parents because they all come within the European Community's definition of 'family'. A British citizen living in England, for example, does not have the automatic right. To marry a non-European Community national, he has first to satisfy the primary purpose rule – rule 50 – in the immigration rules. He has to prove that the primary purpose of the marriage is not for his spouse to gain admission to this country... If he wishes his family to join him, there are even greater and more formidable hurdles... Furthermore, some

British citizens have to satisfy the authorities that they are related to their children.[36]

Third country nationals resident in the EC

After entry to another member state an EC national has extensive protection against discrimination under Community law, together with various benefits to encourage full integration. These include mutual recognition of qualifications, protection under labour laws, entitlement to local rates of social security and other benefits, and free tuition for children; the European Commission has also proposed giving such migrants voting rights in local elections.[37]

Workers who are resident in an EC country but are not EC nationals are reliant on national laws only, which in many cases relegate them to second-class status with minimal rights in such areas as protection from discrimination and access to social security, health and welfare benefits. 1992 will not abolish national requirements for them to obtain and renew work or residence permits. The Social Charter (Chapter Five) seems unlikely to improve their position; the most that is proposed in its Action Programme is a non-binding Memorandum (due to be considered in 1991) on the 'social integration' of migrants from non-EC countries. This will 'lay stress on the quality of administrative and social services afforded to migrants, especially in fields such as education and housing'.[38] The Commission says that this issue 'should be the subject of a wide-ranging debate with the circles concerned'.[39]

On the question of freedom of movement across internal borders the position of third country nationals living in the EC remains undefined, since Commission proposals on the subject relate exclusively to the nationals of member states. The Schengen Convention allows non-EC nationals to travel within the Schengen group for only three months (see above). However, the European Commission has so far failed to grasp this nettle, despite being repeatedly urged to do so by the European Parliament; one argument is that since the issue was not listed as 'essential' in the Palma Document, the Commission has no mandate to tackle it. However, there is speculation that an initiative on equal treatment for non-EC nationals will emerge at European Council level, during the Italian presidency in the second half of 1990.

Meanwhile the British Government's attitude remains predictably negative;[40] in a Commons debate on the Commission's proposals,[4] Douglas Hurd said: '...nothing in the Single European Act conferred the right of free movement on non-EC citizens. That is our clear view, but others in the European Community hold a different legal view...'[11] What Mr Hurd failed to add was that, as we have seen, many long-standing UK residents (most of them citizens of Commonwealth countries) and even some categories of British citizen will not be able to move freely within the EC unless they have acquired full British citizenship.

Immigrants from outside the EC

We have seen earlier in this chapter that the Palma Document (Appendix I) envisages various measures to strengthen the external frontiers of the Community, including common visa requirements (or even a European visa) and a common list of persons to be refused entry. The visa requirements in particular will restrict even further the entry of immigrants in search of work, since the countries on the visa list are likely to be just those poorer countries from which such immigrants have always come. There could thus be an extension of the visa requirement to those Commonwealth citizens who at present can enter Britain without one.

Internal controls

In the 1989 Commons debate on border controls Douglas Hurd said: 'We certainly would not quarrel with member states that have long land frontiers if they wish to operate their checks on non-EC nationals in their cities or workplaces.'[41] This is precisely what happens already in many countries, including Britain, and 1992 could make it much worse. There is ample evidence to suggest that unless proper safeguards are devised there will be increased harassment after 1992 of anyone who is black or a member of a 'visible minority' in an EC country. Such groups already face a much higher risk than others of being stopped and searched by the police.

In Britain there are already raids of homes and workplaces by the police and immigration officers in which whole groups are detained in order to seek out illegal immigrants (technically 'overstayers' and 'illegal entrants'). Black people detained by the police for any reason are liable to have their immigration status queried.[42] Those administering welfare benefits may ask similar questions.[43]

National identity cards are used in some countries as an aid to internal control. Where identity cards are either required or customary, it is black and minority groups that tend to be asked for them. We examine this issue in detail in Chapter Three.

Increased harassment of black people is not an inevitable consequence of 1992, but in the context of legal and institutional discrimination against third country nationals living in the Community it seems very likely. Black people who are full British citizens may suffer discrimination not only at home but when they exercise their right to freedom of movement in the Community. Unless the problem is squarely faced, 1992 can only produce even worse race relations than already exist in much of Europe.

Reversing the trend

There is no shortage of suggestions for avoiding most of the undesirable side-effects of 1992; the problem is to get those in power to take them seriously. A number of manifestos have been drawn up, and some of them are listed below. First, it is worth looking at what the European Parliament has resolved in an attempt to spell out how 1992 must evolve in order to honour the Community's existing commitments, as embodied in the joint Declaration Against Racism and Xenophobia[44] (for full text see Appendix II). The discrepancy between this document and the trends described above is only too obvious.

In a wide-ranging resolution dated 14 February 1989 the European Parliament drew the attention of the Commission, Council and member states to their joint declaration and to the inconsistency of proceeding with a Community policy that allowed, and even encouraged, discrimination. It went on to make specific proposals:

- Freedom of movement should apply to all resident workers irrespective of nationality, with the same rights of family unity as migrant workers who are EC nationals.
- All residents of a member state who are not EC nationals should enjoy the same protection from discrimination in employment and social matters as migrants who are EC nationals.
- The relaxation of border controls should not become an excuse for extensive internal immigration controls aimed at black and ethnic minority communities.
- New visa requirements should not be aimed at excluding people previously admitted freely to a member state from a third country because of historic links between those countries.
- All migrant workers and their families living and working in a member state should be given the right to vote in local elections, whether they are EC nationals or not.[45]

Refugee and immigrant manifestos

Amnesty International has published an International Code of Practice for fair treatment of refugees in the UK.[25] It reinforces the Geneva Convention with specific safeguards against discrimination and arbitrary refusal of refugee status, and calls for asylum-seekers to be presented on arrival with a pamphlet in their own language which explains the procedures to be followed and their rights within those procedures. Amnesty insists on the need for an independent appeal body (something also proposed by the European Commission but never adopted).

The Refugee Forum has published a Refugee Charter for Europe. Its six main demands are as follows:

- those granted asylum should have equal rights with EC nationals regarding movement, work and political activity;
- immediate entitlement to welfare benefits for asylum-seekers;
- independent appeals with legal rights for those facing deportation, detention or repatriation;
- the right to seek employment and/or study if an appeal takes longer than three months;
- permanent residence for refugees and those with 'exceptional leave to remain' (a kind of second-class status with no security) after four years, with a right of appeal if refused;
- the offer to all asylum seekers of a directory in all relevant languages giving details of advisory and advocacy services, with a guaranteed right to contact such services.[14]

The Refugee Council (formerly the British Refugee Council) has also published a Refugee Manifesto supported by a range of interested groups. Its ten demands cover similar ground to the two manifestos mentioned above, with the following additions:

- asylum-seekers should not be prevented from reaching Britain by visa restrictions and fines on airlines;
- immigration officers should have special training in human rights issues;
- no asylum-seeker should be held in detention;
- asylum-seekers and refugees should have the right to be joined by their immediate family;
- governments and the EC should consult and give funding to community groups and agencies working with refugees.[46]

Manifestos covering both immigrants and refugees have also been published by the Refugee Forum and Migrant Rights Action Network[14] and by other groups.[47] These include the following points:

- abolition of visa controls based on race;
- the right of third-country nationals resident in EC countries to live and work in any EC country on an equal footing with EC nationals;
- no restriction on rights of entry of relatives of third-country nationals resident in the EC;
- family reunion not to be subject to employment or accommodation qualifications;

- all children born in an EC country to have the right to nationality of that country;
- women's right to stay not to be linked to that of husbands and families;
- an end to internal passport and immigration checks on black residents;
- legal protection from discrimination and the granting of full civic, welfare and political rights for all EC residents regardless of nationality;
- an amnesty for those living and working in EC countries in breach of immigration laws. This is particularly relevant to refugees who fail to apply for asylum in fear of being refused and sent home.

Conclusion

The various refugee and immigrant manifestos speak for themselves in pointing to the racism and discrimination already facing refugees and immigrants, and their justified fears concerning the impact of 1992. The European Parliament has clearly recognised the contrast between the EC's solemn declarations and the apparent reality of its intentions, but the Commission and especially the Council (where the real power lies) seem determined to ignore this contradiction. The opportunity to address decades of discriminatory practices throughout Europe, and to prevent them from becoming more entrenched in the context of 1992, is in danger of being lost.

Notes

1. In this respect the authorities were no doubt aware that many criminals (including terrorists) originate within the Community. In West Germany, for instance, almost half the people detained at intra-Community borders are nationals or residents of Community states. See House of Lords Select Committee on the European Communities, *1992: Border Controls of People*, Session 1988-89, 22nd Report (HMSO, 1989), Evidence p. 189.
2. Alan Butt Philip, *European Border Controls: Who Needs Them?* (Royal Institute of International Affairs, London, 1989), p. 23.
3. House of Lords Select Committee on the European Communities, *1992: Border Controls of People*, Session 1988-89, 22nd Report (HMSO, 1989), Report Appendix 5.
4. *Ibid*., Report Appendix 4; this reproduces the Commission proposal, *Communication of the Commission to the Council on the Abolition of Controls of Persons at Intra-Community Borders*, COM (88) 640 (European Commission, Brussels, 1988).
5. For the text of the 1985 Schengen Agreement see House of Lords Select Committee on the European Communities, *1992 Border Controls of People*,

Session 1988-89, 22nd Report (HMSO, 1989), Report Appendix 3. For a more detailed account see the appendix by C.A. Groenendijk in Paul Gordon, *Fortress Europe? The Meaning of 1992* (Runnymede Trust, London, 1989), pp. 31-9.

6. David Usborne, 'Clear from Biarritz to Berlin', in *The Independent on Sunday*, 17 June 1990.
7. *Official Journal of the European Communities*, C323 (27 December 1989), pp. 98-9.
8. José J. Bolten, 'The right to seek asylum in Europe', in *Netherlands Quarterly on Human Rights* 4/1989, pp. 381-412.
9. *Hansard*, 4 May 1989, col. 396.
10. *Daily Mail*, 18 May 1989.
11. Home Office, *Explanatory Memorandum on European Community Document*, 10412/88 (1989). See also House of Commons Home Affairs Committee, *Practical Police Co-operation in the European Community*, Session 1989-90, Memoranda of Evidence pp. 9-10.
12. *Hansard*, 4 May 1989, col. 399.
13. House of Lords Select Committee on the European Communities, *1992: Border Controls of People*, Session 1988-89, 22nd Report (HMSO, 1989), Evidence pp. 103-9. The latest UK statistics on refugees (*Home Office Statistical Bulletin*, Issue 22/90) show that in 1989 the number of applicants for refugee status in the UK rose to 15,500, of whom 3,000 were granted asylum.
14. Refugee Forum and Migrant Rights Action Network, *The Migrant and Refugee Manifesto* (Refugee Forum, London, 1989).
15. Richard Plender, *International Migration Law*, 2nd Edn (Nijhoff, 1988), Ch. 12.
16. *The Independent*, 7 March 1990.
17. *Ibid.*, 22 January 1990; *JCWI Bulletin* (Joint Council for the Welfare of Immigrants, London), 4 February 1990.
18. Richard Plender, *International Migration Law*, 2nd Edn (Nijhoff, 1988), pp. 227-36; see also Nicholas Blake, 'Life after the Lords: developments in the case of Sivakumaran and others', *Immigration and Nationality Law and Practice*, January 1990, pp. 7-10.
19. Paul Gordon, *Fortress Europe? The Meaning of 1992* (Runnymede Trust, London, 1989), pp. 14-15.
20. Ad Hoc Group on Immigration, *Declaration by the Ministers Concerned with Immigration*, WGI 513 (December 1989); copy deposited with Parliament.

21. H. Vetter (rapporteur), *Report on the Right of Asylum*, Documents A2-227/86/A & B (European Parliament, 1986); see also *Official Journal of the European Communities*, C99 (13 April 1987), pp. 167-71 for adoption of the report and *ibid*., C190 (20 July 1987), p. 105 for a further resolution.
22. Philip Rudge, in H. Vetter (rapporteur), *Report on the Right of Asylum*, Part B, Document A2-227/86/B (European Parliament, 1986), pp. 109-12; also *Towards Harmonization of Refugee Policies in Europe? A Contribution to the Discussion* (European Consultation on Refugees and Exiles, London, 1988).
23. House of Lords Select Committee on the European Communities, *1992: Border Controls of People*, Session 1988-89, 22nd Report (HMSO, 1989), Evidence pp. 161-3.
24. *Ibid*., Evidence pp. 36-50; also *Unequal Migrants: The European Community's Unequal Treatment of Migrants and Refugees* (Joint Council for the Welfare of Immigrants, London, 1989).
25. *Exiled: Asylum Seekers in the UK* (Amnesty International British Section, London, 1988).
26. House of Lords Select Committee on the European Communities, *1992: Border Controls of People*, Session 1988-89, 22nd Report (HMSO, 1989), Evidence pp. 51-6.
27. *1992 and the Black Community*, report of conference in Birmingham, June 1989 (KAAMYABI, Leeds, 1989).
28. Edward Mayo, *Beyond 1992: the Effect of the Single European Market on the World's Poor* (World Development Movement, London, 1989).
29. Gil Loescher, *International Affairs*, Vol. 65 (1989) pp. 617-36.
30. David Buchan and John Wyles, 'The intolerance threshold nears', in *Financial Times*, 12 March 1990.
31. *Informal Consultation Meeting on Migrants from Non-EEC Countries in the Single European Market after 1992*, Informal Summary Record (International Labour Office, Geneva, 1989), Appendix 6.
32. *British Nationality: the New Act* (Joint Council for the Welfare of Immigrants, London, 1986).
33. Regulation 1612/68, amended by Regulation 312/76; also Directive 68/360.
34. For a full discussion and background information see House of Lords Select Committee on the European Communities, *Free Movement of People and Right of Residence in the European Community*, Session 1989-90, 7th Report (HMSO, 1990).
35. *Ibid*., Report p. 8.
36. *Hansard*, 8 February 1990, cols 1104-6.

37. For Commission documents and other material see House of Lords Select Committee on the European Communities, *Voting Rights in Local Elections*, Session 1989-90, 6th Report (HMSO, 1990).
38. *Communication from the Commission Concerning its Action Programme Relating to the Implementation of the Community Charter of Basic Social Rights for Workers*, COM (89) 568 final (European Commission, Brussels, 1989), p. 20.
39. *Ibid.*, p. 17.
40. *Explanatory Memorandum on European Community Document* (Home Office, July 1989).
41. *Hansard*, 4 May 1989, col. 398.
42. Paul Gordon, *Policing Immigration: Britain's Internal Controls* (Pluto, 1985), pp. 23-6 and 51-7.
43. *Ibid.*, pp. 89-94.
44. *Official Journal of the European Communities*, C158 (25 June 1986), pp. 1-3.
45. *Ibid.*, C69 (20 March 1989), pp. 40-4.
46. *Refugee Manifesto*, published for the 1989 European Elections (British Refugee Council, London, 1989).
47. See for example, *Communities of Resistance Conference Pack* (Hackney Council Race Relations Unit, 1989); also *Whose Europe?*, ed. Dave Cook and Paul Gordon (Refugee Forum, London, 1989).

CHAPTER THREE

Information and Big Brother

Orwell's *Nineteen Eighty-Four* envisaged a society in which every detail of a citizen's activities was monitored and recorded by the agents of Big Brother. Orwell foresaw that advances in technology would make this progressively easier. Government data banks of personal data (or 'name-linked data') are now expanding rapidly all over the developed world, and the police and other agencies show an unquenchable thirst for more storage and exchange of information.[1] These developments clearly facilitate any measure to control society. Will 1992 increase the dangers to civil liberties inherent in such a trend?

Until recently the nations of the EC had not devoted much attention to the issue; the emphasis had been on facilitating, rather than regulating, the exchange of information in the interests of an efficient internal market. In the European Commission, a whole directorate (DG XIII) is devoted to telecommunications and the 'information industries', but data protection has only been a minor feature of its work.

A related issue is the possibility of exercising increased control over people within the Community by means of identity cards and associated central data banks. Here data protection concerns overlap the wider issues of police powers and internal controls (see Chapters Two and Four).

This chapter starts by examining the general problem of data protection in the Community. We then examine the particular issue of identity cards. Are they, as some people insist, accepted throughout the Continent? If they do come to Britain, what are the likely effects? Is there really no alternative to their introduction if internal frontiers are to be abolished? Such questions need to be addressed alongside those concerning data protection; in both cases the privacy and other civil liberties of the individual are at stake.

Data protection

It has been recognised for some time that there is a potentially serious conflict between the aims of the 1992 process and the need to protect the privacy of individuals regarding personal data. With the explosive growth of the 'information market', involving the development of radically new technologies (see below), individual countries have been presented with quite enough problems; with trans-border information exchanges increasing as well, the task of overall regulation becomes far more complex. The potential threat to an individual's privacy can therefore arise not only in his or her own country, but also in another country to which data are transmitted. This can occur as a result of data transfers between private organisations, between the agencies of different governments, or a combination of these (as in the use of electoral rolls for direct marketing, for example).

The Council of Europe Convention

European countries vary widely in the degree of data protection that is available. In an effort to encourage harmonisation, the non-EC Council of Europe (see Chapter One) drew up its Convention for the Protection of Individuals with Regard to Automatic Processing of Personal Data in 1981. This encourages the free flow of data between countries, but allows for the prohibition of data transfer where the recipient country does not have equivalent protection or where the data may be re-exported to a country that has not adopted the Convention.

As its title indicates, the Convention covers personal information but applies only to automated (computerised) data; however, there is an option to extend coverage to manual files. The Convention has the force of law among the contracting parties, but unlike the corresponding Convention on Human Rights (see Chapter Six) there is no right of individual petition in cases of abuse – a weakness which is discussed below.

The Convention calls for contracting parties to enact laws which incorporate its principles and to appoint national authorities whose task is to facilitate mutual assistance on data protection. In response to this the British Government, which signed the Convention in 1981, drew up proposals which led to the Data Protection Act 1984 and the appointment of an independent Data Protection Registrar. The Registrar keeps a register of users of computerised data, who are obliged (with exceptions) to declare various particulars such as the source of the data and the purpose of collecting it. The Registrar also investigates breaches of the Act (either independently or after a complaint) and monitors the relevance of the Act to new technical developments. The Act follows the specific principles of the Convention but refrains from taking up wider options such as the inclusion of manual files. The basic principles, as outlined in Article 5 of the Convention, are that personal data shall be:

- obtained and processed fairly and lawfully;
- stored for specified and legitimate purposes and not used in a way incompatible with those purposes;
- adequate, relevant and not excessive in relation to the purposes for which they are stored;
- accurate and, where necessary, kept up to date; and
- preserved in a form which permits identification of the data subjects for no longer than is required for the purpose for which those data are stored.

In 1981 the European Commission issued a strong Recommendation that all member states should sign and ratify the Council of Europe Convention.[2] The Commission added that if this was not done 'within a reasonable time' it reserved the right to press for a mandatory instrument (e.g. a Directive) to be adopted by the EC's Council. Nine years later (1990) the position is that only six of the 12 EC states which have signed the Convention have ratified it, a step involving parliamentary approval and a detailed commitment to implementation. Spain is in the apparently anomalous position of having ratified the Convention without passing the relevant laws, but claims that there is broad protection under its national constitution; specific legislation is still under discussion.

In four cases (Belgium, Greece, Italy and Portugal) the failure to ratify is related to the absence so far of national laws on data protection, though the first three countries have legislation drafted, and Portugal now has a data protection clause in its constitution.[3] Ireland and the Netherlands have appropriate legislation and intend to ratify soon. The situation in the wider Council of Europe grouping is worse, with only nine of the 23 states having ratified the Convention.[3]

This confusion and lack of common purpose have clearly alarmed the data protection authorities in those countries without data protection laws. At the international conference of data protection commissioners (equivalent to Britain's Registrar) in August 1989, a resolution was passed drawing attention to the problems involved in transmitting personal data across borders. If the states concerned do not have equivalent legal safeguards, '...there can be no guarantee that the data are up to date, accurate, and used only for proper purposes; and the individual loses the opportunity to appeal to any data protection commissioner.'[4]

The commissioners went on to assert their belief that 'data protection should be given the same priority as the promotion of data processing and telecommunications in the development and use of international data services';[4] in other words, it is no good setting up new data exchange networks and only then considering protection of data from misuse. The only answer, they say, is for governments to move rapidly towards establishing equivalent legal safeguards as soon as possible.

At the same conference, the data protection commissioners of the EC states agreed an additional statement that pointed to a new danger:

> On a growing scale, personal information data bases are maintained by the European Community institutions themselves. However, these institutions are not subject to data protection legislation and hence to any requirement to meet the Basic Principles for Data Protection.[4]

The basic principles referred to are those laid down in the Convention and in a similar set of guidelines drawn up by the Organisation for Economic Co-operation and Development (OECD), and the data bases in question are those used to compile statistical reports.[5] In agriculture, for instance, individuals are not identified in the statistics but the Community's data files may well contain 'name-linked data'.

A further problem is that an absence of data protection in certain states may turn them into 'data havens' where information can be processed free of restrictions.[6] This raises justified fears about the whole idea of encouraging EC-wide information exchange. To address these questions the data protection commissioners' statement made two proposals: that 'appropriate legal instruments' should ensure that the basic principles in the Convention are binding on all member nations and on the EC institutions themselves, and that an independent data protection authority should be established to supervise data processing within the EC institutions and co-operate with national data protection bodies.[4]

This last proposal would follow the precedent set by the Council of Europe, which now has a data protection commissioner to supervise its own handling of data. However, such reforms stop short of creating a supranational data protection body.

Options facing the Community

For some years now the European Commission has been wrestling with the problem of which option to press for in its attempt to bring dilatory member states into line on data protection. The weakest option, that of a non-binding Recommendation to member states, would only repeat the 1981 process that signally failed. The toughest option, that of a Directive to member states to bring their laws into line with the Convention, had until recently been shelved (see below). There are further problems to resolve, as a member of the European Commission staff told the assembled data protection commissioners in 1989:

- Should a Community initiative merely accelerate the process of ratifying the Convention, or should it go beyond that on the basis of specific Community requirements?
- Should it be combined with a freedom of information initiative?
- Should there be 'sectoral' initiatives covering each field of application (e.g. separate moves on data of economic relevance as opposed to police data and other sensitive categories), either in parallel with a general initiative or on their own?[6]

A powerful new incentive for Community action emerged when the immigration ministers of the EC states involved in the Working Group on Immigration (see

Chapter Two) issued a declaration following their meeting in Paris in December 1989. This included the following statement:

> In order effectively to implement visa policy and the jointly defined controls along our external borders, we feel it essential that we should begin to exchange information about persons who must be refused access to the territories of one of our Member States on the grounds that their presence there could threaten security or public order in one of our States and we have decided to look into the best ways of doing this, with special reference to computerization. We undertake that this exchange of information can be envisaged only if beforehand a legal framework guaranteeing the protection of individual liberties and privacy has been established.[7]

In making this last statement, the ministers concerned were clearly aware of the concern already expressed by data protection commissioners about the implications of the Schengen Information System,[4] under which there would be circulation of information about a wide range of individuals (see Chapter Two). They no doubt also took into account the warning given by the European Commission's Legal Advisory Board, that in the absence of uniform data protection within the Community, a member state would be justified in prohibiting the transfer of data to those states without equivalent protection.[8]

It was therefore no surprise when the Commission announced in March 1990 that the idea of a data protection Directive had been reactivated after lying dormant for a number of years, with the aim of submitting a draft to the Council of Ministers as soon as possible. Since the prime concern of the immigration ministers is not data protection but information exchange, it was feared that pressure would be exerted to accept a minimum standard of protection consistent with ensuring this exchange. However, the various data protection commissioners made it clear that they would not countenance any lowering of standards, and there are indications that this warning has been heeded. The Commission's draft proposals are discussed later in the chapter.

Any detailed proposals will need to be examined very closely from the civil liberty point of view. As in other areas, the key question will be whether harmonisation is to be 'upwards' (towards the highest protection for individuals) or 'downwards'. A cynic might conclude that the prospects are rather better for data protection than they are (say) for refugees, since in the former case there are powerful commercial interests in favour of a high level of protection for any data transmitted across borders.

Existing variations in data protection

The scope for 'upwards' or 'downwards' harmonisation is apparent when one compares the existing or proposed data protection laws of EC states with the Council of Europe Convention and the OECD guidelines. We discuss here only the former, since the OECD guidelines are broadly similar to the provisions of the Convention and in some respects less precise.

As mentioned above, the Convention only covers automated data but offers a member state the option (under Article 3) of applying the rules to manual files containing personal data. Among the EC states, four have taken up this option (Denmark, France, West Germany and the Netherlands) and two intend to do so (Greece, Portugal); the remaining six states have not.[9] In Britain the exclusion of manual files has emerged as a major loophole allowing circumvention of the principles of the Convention, as in the activities of the Economic League; this private vetting agency supplies employers with confidential information about prospective employees and keeps the information on manual files to which the persons listed have no legal right of access.[10] In view of the precedent now set, however, by the Schengen Convention and the new European Asylum Convention (see Chapter Two), the continued exclusion from the Data Protection Act of all manual files will become increasingly anomalous.

A further concern is the provision made in Article 3 of the Convention allowing a state to exclude from protection (subject only to its domestic law) any categories of personal data which it thinks fit, the only requirement being that a list of such categories will be deposited with the Secretary General of the Council of Europe. Furthermore, Article 9 allows derogation from all the safeguards provided for the individual (access to data, correction of mistakes and so on) when it is in the interests of 'protecting State security, public safety, the monetary interests of the State or the suppression of criminal offences'. Britain has a similar provision built into the Data Protection Act (see below), although no formal derogation has been lodged with the Council of Europe.

This naturally leads to variations between states, and is the area where harmonisation seems most likely to lead to a longer list of exclusions than that applying in any one country at present; the phrase 'protecting State security' evokes a strong response in ministerial minds, and no government is likely to volunteer to abandon any of its exclusions.

In the case of the UK, Section 27 of the Data Protection Act gives a blanket exemption from the provisions of the Act to personal data 'if the exemption is required for the purpose of safeguarding national security'. This requires only the signature of a government minister (not specified), and exempts the data user from even registering the existence of the files with the Data Protection Registrar. Furthermore, even registered data may lose the normal safeguard against unauthorised disclosure (Section 15 of the Act) if a minister signs an appropriate certificate. Such certificates ensure that people whose names are on MI5 files cannot find out what is recorded about them.

The Act also gives a list of data categories to which the 'data subject' (the person to whom the data relate) cannot automatically gain access, correct errors or claim compensation for loss of the data or unauthorised disclosure.[11] These categories include data held for the prevention or detection of crime, the apprehension or prosecution of offenders, and assessment or collection of a tax or duty. However, the data user has to show (before a court if necessary) that either subject access or non-disclosure would be 'likely to prejudice' the prevention of crime and so on; a case-by-case justification is required.

The same 'prejudice' rule on subject access applies to personal data obtained from a person who had the information for one of the purposes listed above, and which are 'held for the purpose of discharging statutory functions'. This means that data collected under an Act of Parliament may be excluded from subject access.

Other EC countries vary widely in their treatment of excluded categories; some exclude files such as police files from any subject access, while in France there is provision for the data protection authority to check and correct a file on a person's behalf where 'national security', defence or public safety are involved.

Another source of variation relates to the requirement under Article 6 of the Convention: 'Personal data revealing racial origin, political opinions or religious or other beliefs, as well as personal data concerning health or sexual life, may not be processed automatically unless domestic law provides appropriate safeguards. The same shall apply to personal data relating to criminal convictions.'[11] This is a major source of concern which has been recognised in a Council of Europe Recommendation on data held by the police (see below), and also in the new Schengen Convention (see Chapter Two).

France's data protection law prohibits the recording (or storage in a computer memory) of personal data reflecting racial origins or political, philosophical or religious opinions or union membership, unless the person concerned has given express consent; the only exception is the membership records of churches, unions and so on. Other countries allow such data to be recorded under certain restrictions. Britain's Data Protection Act has a provision under Section 2(3) for the Home Secretary to lay down safeguards for such sensitive data by making statutory orders; however, this power has never yet been exercised. Furthermore, the UK entered specific reservations on the Council of Europe's Recommendations covering sensitive police and social security data (see below).

File linkage and personal identifiers

One of the most important differences between countries lies in their attitudes towards the linkage or interconnection of data files held by government departments and agencies, and the related question of assigning a national identity number to each individual. We discuss below (in connection with identity cards) the reservations expressed on this score by Britain's Data Protection Registrar; they mirror the fears voiced in connection with new technologies (see below), that linkage of files makes it possible to build up a composite picture of an individual without his or her knowledge. Britain's Data Protection Act does not specifically prohibit this; the holder of a file has only to deposit with the Registrar a list of those to whom the data may be disclosed and satisfy the Registrar that the data protection principles listed in the Act will not be contravened.

At government level the linkage of files is being actively facilitated by the new Government Data Network. This privately-operated system was initially planned to link the Home Office, Customs and Excise, Inland Revenue and Health and Social Security departments, but this was just the beginning; the Home Secretary said in 1988 that he was considering linking in the Police National Computer,[12] and there is no limit to the possible expansion of the network. The Data Protection Registrar has announced his intention of discussing with the Government the drawing up of 'some statement of the circumstances and disciplines governing any exchange of personal data between them [i.e. government departments]'.[13] The Government insists that the network is intended mostly for data exchanges within each department, but there is no guarantee that this will remain the case as the system develops. In a 1989 report, the Government's own National Audit Office noted: 'There appear to be no clearly available standard procedures governing the exchange of information between departments, by the Government Data Network or any other means'.[14]

In other countries the possible dangers have been taken more seriously, and the scene may be set for another disagreement between Britain and its Community partners. Portugal's new constitution forbids the interconnection of files save in exceptional cases, and it is laid down that 'citizens shall not be given all-purpose national identification numbers'.[3] Greece has instituted a system of national identity numbers for certain public sector data files, but the linkage of these files is forbidden by law.[15]

Outside Europe, the Canadian government has taken steps to prevent the Social Insurance Number from becoming a universal personal identifier; at considerable cost, a separate employee identifier is being introduced for federal employees, and the matching-up of computer files is being reduced.[16] In Australia, the Privacy Act 1988 forbids the use of the tax file number as a national identification system 'by whatever means'. Similar moves have been started in the USA, where the Social Security Number has tended to be treated as a universal identifier.[17]

In Britain, although a national identity card and number have been rejected for the time being (see below), there is nonetheless potential for a universal identifier to be introduced by stealth; the Inland Revenue has for some time been using the National Insurance Number to identify taxpayers. Poll tax registration data could also be used to develop a universal identifier.

New technologies

New technologies seem certain to complicate the task of achieving comprehensive protection of personal data throughout the EC and, as in other areas, there are wide variations between countries in the level of protection offered. Those who deal with the legal aspects of data protection are engaged in an ongoing race to keep up with new developments. Definitions which seemed to cover all types of data processing in 1981, when the Council of Europe Convention was drawn up, are no longer adequate.

This emerges clearly from the Council of Europe's report on new technologies issued in 1989; the experts who wrote the report acknowledge at the beginning that the categories of new technology listed in their 1985 terms of reference are already out of date.[18] Their report is, however, a useful guide to the types of problem that are proliferating in the data protection field. Some examples taken from it will illustrate the problems that need to be tackled.

Telemetry covers the remote reading of water, electricity and gas meters; itemised metering of telephone calls; and monitoring of the television programmes watched by an individual. The remote reading of supply meters might appear innocuous enough, but the report quotes a proposal in Norway to record individual electricity consumption automatically every six minutes; this accumulation of detail is condemned as being 'a real danger for privacy, particularly if data are used for purposes which are incompatible with the original aim'.[19]

The report also groups electronic (sound or video) surveillance under the heading of telemetry. The data protection laws of some countries (but not the UK) are interpreted as covering video surveillance; in West Germany it has been established that video surveillance of employees in the workplace is only legal in exceptional cases.[20] In France the data protection authority takes a similar view, though the issue has not yet been tested in the courts. In the UK the National Council for Civil Liberties (Liberty) has argued strongly for separate legislation to regulate the video surveillance of public places, so as to curb unnecessary surveillance and ensure the confidentiality of recorded tapes.[21]

Interactive media include a wide range of systems through which an individual can consult a data base to obtain information. If the user remains anonymous there is no risk to privacy, but in the videotex type of system the user's actions are recorded by the provider of the service; examples are teleshopping, telebanking, audience response surveys and electronic polling. The report points out that every time an individual uses such a system, information is added to a growing file on the person's actions – what request was made, what decision was taken, where and when the action took place. A 'profile' of the unwitting generator of the data is built up: 'The profile is a marketable commodity in itself but the element of control or surveillance of users which such a technique permits is perhaps a more alarming possibility.'[22] The report argues that this is particularly dangerous when the collector of information is a state-controlled body.

The report refers only briefly to new possibilities being opened up by the creation of transmission systems which integrate previously separate services, such as the Integrated Services Digital Network (ISDN) which links telephone, telex and data processing through the common use of 'digitised' data: speech, telex messages, computer data and even pictures can now be reduced to sequences of 'bits' of information that can all be transmitted by the same means. Television networks can be incorporated to create Integrated Broadband Communications (IBC). The report reflects a measure of dismay at the task of legislating in an area where information which can circulate freely (such as television programmes) is mixed with personal data that may be confidential.

The authors recognise (without offering a solution) that the rapid spread of interactive and remote-monitoring techniques is leading to an alarming prospect: 'In fact, there is from now on the possibility of total surveillance of the individual. In addition, information is today being circulated, disseminated and dispersed in conditions which make it more and more difficult to protect.'[23] 1992 gives a new urgency to the search for solutions.

Guidelines for harmonisation

As in the broader field of human rights, the Council of Europe has augmented its basic Convention with a series of formal Recommendations on particular areas of data protection; these 'sectoral recommendations' have been adopted by the Council's Committee of Ministers, and countries that have ratified the Convention are expected to follow them unless a reservation is entered at the time of adoption – though there is no mechanism for enforcing compliance.

The Recommendations are also influential in countries which have not yet passed data protection legislation. They provide a useful framework for discussing harmonisation among EC states, and could form the basis of EC Directives enforceable by the European Court of Justice – an arrangement preferable to relying on voluntary compliance, particularly in cases where government agencies may be tempted to depart from the rules. Recent examples which aim to protect 'name-linked data' from misuse are as follows:

- R (81) 1 on automated medical data banks;
- R (83) 10 on statistical and research data;
- R (85) 20 on direct marketing;
- R (86) 1 on personal data used for social security purposes;
- R (87) 15 on the use of personal data in the police sector;
- R (89) 2 on personal data used for employment purposes;
- R (89) 14 on ethical issues of HIV infection (including data confidentiality).[24]

All of these relate to personal privacy, and some (such as that on police data) are relevant to other civil liberties. The Recommendation on employment data is taken seriously by companies operating across international borders, since they have a clear interest in satisfying the data protection authorities in all the countries in which they operate.

The British Government has entered formal reservations on two of the above Recommendations. On R (86) 1 (social security data), the Government reserves the right 'to comply or not' with three sentences in the text. One of these (part of Principle 1. 2) defines the welfare and other benefits covered by the term 'social security'. The second (in Principle 3.3) requires the consent of the person concerned to the obtaining of sensitive data from other sources. The third sentence objected to is Principle 5.1, which says: 'The introduction or use of a single uniform social security number or similar means of identification should be accompanied by adequate safeguards provided for by domestic law.'

On R (87) 15 (police data), the Government entered reservations on two items: one ensuring that individuals are ultimately informed that information recorded without their knowledge is still in the file (Principle 2.2), and another (Principle 2.4) which reads as follows:

> The collection of data on individuals solely on the basis that they have a particular racial origin, particular religious convictions, sexual behaviour or political opinions or belong to particular movements or organisations which are not proscribed by law should be prohibited. The collection of data concerning these factors may only be carried out if absolutely necessary for the purposes of a particular enquiry.

As mentioned above, Britain's Data Protection Act contains only a latent power to limit the use of such data, and no use has so far been made of it. Britain was the only Council of Europe nation to enter specific reservations on the clauses described above.

Police files in Britain

The UK's failure to endorse the whole of the Council of Europe's Recommendation R (87) 15 on police data is particularly serious in view of the imminence of Community-wide data exchange systems for police and immigration services (see Chapter Four). The Council of Europe has issued clear guidelines on the interpretation of the Recommendation, and these are quite specific on the issue of sensitive data:

> It may be the case that the collection of certain sensitive data will be necessary... However, in no circumstances should such data be collected *simply* in order to allow the police to compile a file on certain minority groups whose behaviour or conduct is within the law.[25]

The signatories of the five-nation Schengen Convention (see Chapter Two) accepted that R (87) 15 should be adhered to in operating the Schengen Information System, and the same Convention specifically forbids the recording of sensitive data as defined in Article 6 of the Council of Europe Convention (see above). The same principles have been accepted in a recent document on police co-operation issued by the ministers of the Trevi Group of EC states (see Chapter One); R (87) 15 is again cited as a guide to be followed.[26]

The current guidelines for the British police service, issued in 1987 by the Association of Chief Police Officers (ACPO), and not so far revised, make no reference to the issue of sensitive data, nor to R (87) 15; they relate only to the principles spelt out in the Data Protection Act 1984.[27] This is worrying, in that R (87) 15 (even subject to the reservations mentioned above) implicitly discourages a practice that is common in Britain – the disclosure of police records on individuals to a wide range of government and other agencies, for the purpose of pre-employment vetting. This may involve disclosing not only past convictions, but local police records concerning the individual. The practice was tacitly sanctioned by the Data Protection Registrar when he allowed the police to register as data users with the following blanket exemption:

> Because of the nature of the purpose, other sources or disclosures, including any on the Registrar's list, may be used or made in connection with particular enquiries.[28]

The wording of R (87) 15 is much more precise; communication of data is generally permissible only if, *in a particular case*, there is a clear legal obligation or authorisation, or in the same case the communication has been authorised by the supervisory authority (i.e. the Data Protection Registrar).[25] There are additional conditions allowing communication of data to other public bodies, but transfer to 'private bodies' is allowed only if the subject of the data consents, or if a 'serious and imminent danger' is to be prevented.

The Registrar admitted to the House of Commons Home Affairs Committee that the current lack of guidance in the UK placed the police in a difficult position when deciding who should be given access to police records on an individual. The committee commented:

> The fact that 51 police forces might permit access in a haphazard and unaccountable manner has worrying implications for the liberty of the individual. We believe that if the public were more aware of these arrangements, there would be an outcry.[29]

The situation certainly seems to be in need of regulation: the Home Affairs Committee found to its surprise that, in 1989 alone, over half a million people had had their police records checked in pre-employment security vetting by government departments and approved agencies. The committee also expressed alarm at the admitted level of inaccuracies in criminal records.[30] In the field of employment involving work with children (see below), another half million checks were made over a similar one-year period.[31]

There are undoubtedly difficulties in balancing the need to protect individual privacy against the wider interests of vulnerable groups such as children, and these will increase as 1992 approaches. Home Office Circular No. 102/1988 says that where official bodies are recruiting staff who will have access to children, the police may disclose details of past convictions and other information, even where no proceedings were taken; Circular No. 58/1989 sets out comparable rules for the voluntary sector. To protect the interests of children, information of this kind will need to be exchanged between countries when individuals travel abroad in search of work; at the same time there will need to be procedures that prevent any leakage of data into the wrong hands.

Information without frontiers

The Council of Europe report on new technologies becomes most pessimistic in the area of data transmission across national borders.[32] It is now possible, for example, for trans-border flow to include the use by individuals of portable computers plugged into telephone sockets, so that information is exchanged with data bases in other countries. What national or international law can regulate such activities? The authors of the report have this to say:

> ...as the volume of trans-border flow increases, the control possibilities diminish. It becomes much more difficult, for example, to identify the countries through which data will transit before reaching the authorised recipient. Problems of data security and confidentiality are heightened

> when data are piped through communication lines which traverse countries where little or no attention is accorded to issues of data protection. The trans-border flow of sensitive data in particular becomes more acute.[32]

The report illustrates the legal problems with a conundrum:

> It may well be that a data file is stored in country A, the controller of the file is resident in country B, the data subject is domiciled in country C. Which law should apply if, through unauthorised access to the file, damage is caused to the data subject's interests in country D?[32]

The Council of Europe Convention is silent on problems such as this.

A supranational data protection authority?

It is apparent that even large business concerns have good cause to worry about the problems of protecting confidential data transmitted across borders. How much worse is it likely to be for vulnerable individuals with minimal resources and little access to legal assistance? What steps can be taken to safeguard against damaging but inaccurate information being shared by every police force in Europe, with disastrous consequences for an innocent individual? What about refugees who may fear the consequences of information about their whereabouts leaking back to the country from which they fled? Answers to these questions will have to be found, whatever form the new Europe may take.

Until recently there have been few moves towards solving these problems, though the Schengen Convention sets a good example in this respect (but not in others – see Chapter Two). We have seen that a data protection authority for Europe has been mooted, but only with reference to data held by EC institutions; the idea was welcomed by François Mitterand (as President of the Council) and Jacques Delors (President of the Commission).[33]

The real problem is that there is no person or body with the authority to rule on data-protection matters involving more than one country's jurisdiction, and no equivalent of the Commission and Court of Human Rights to which an individual may complain. It appears that there are strong arguments for setting up such institutions without delay and giving them comparable powers of enforcement.

An encouraging move in the right direction has been the revival of the idea of a binding Directive on data protection (see above). Although nothing had been published by August 1990, there were indications that the problem was at last being addressed by devising a wide-ranging set of draft proposals. If accepted, these could set a new and higher standard for data protection throughout the Community. Apart from a proposal dealing with the new technologies of integrated services digital networks (see above) and digital mobile networks, the most important draft Directive was believed at the time of writing to make the following proposals:

- Every member state must have an independent data protection authority with adequate powers of investigation and intervention; it must ensure compliance with national laws based on the Directive and be given access to all relevant files.
- Manual data are to be covered, subject to a rather precise definition of the way in which the data are stored: if *structured and accessible in an organised collection, according to specific criteria so as to facilitate the utilisation or interconnection of data*, then personal data of this kind are to come under the Directive. The data can be either centrally stored or distributed between different sites.
- 'Sensitive data' on racial origin, political opinions, religious or philosophical convictions, trade union membership, health and sexual life are not to be automatically processed without the written consent of the person concerned, unless there is specific derogation by a member state and a national law guaranteeing confidentiality. It is not clear whether this would apply also to manual files.
- In cases where subject access is not guaranteed (e.g. for reasons of 'national security'), the national data protection authority is to check the data on behalf of the person concerned.
- Transmission of personal data (or on-line access) by private organisations is to be subject to prior consent by the person concerned, and the national data protection authority is to be informed of the existence of the data file.
- A supervisory committee is to be set up at Community level, chaired and serviced by the European Commission, to monitor compliance with the Directive; since a Directive is binding on member states, this means that offenders could be penalised under Community law. Members of national data protection authorities will sit on this committee.
- New proposals for data protection are to be put by the European Commission to the supervisory committee and to a second, consultative committee comprising experts from the member states.

The European Commission approved the draft Directive in July 1990 for submission under Article 100a of the Treaty of Rome, as a measure that needs to be achieved by the end of 1992. Such proposals require only a qualified majority vote in the Council.

The detailed proposals (which include others besides those listed above) go well beyond the mandatory provisions of the Council of Europe Convention, and certainly set a higher standard than that currently existing in several EC countries. A Directive of this kind would go some way towards meeting the concerns outlined in this chapter, though many problems would remain. News of the reception given to the draft after it is put to the Council in October 1990 will therefore be awaited with interest, not least in Britain.

Identity cards

As we have seen in Chapter Two, the abolition of internal frontiers is widely assumed to go hand in hand not only with stricter controls on entry at the Community's borders with the rest of the world, but also with increased control over freedom of movement within each member state. This latter aspect of the matter has not been much talked about by governments, since they appreciate only too well that it may prove to be deeply unpopular with their electorates. The European Commission, too, has studiously avoided the subject; when pressed to express an opinion to a 1989 House of Lords inquiry into the effect of abolishing border controls (*1992: Border Controls of People*[34]), a Commission official replied:

> ...those countries which do not currently do so may wish to consider changing their internal surveillance into a tighter system. We are not saying that they should, and it is not in our power to suggest that. But to the extent that we suggest that spot checks at the frontiers should be more a feature of life, if anyone feels that that leaves a gap the implication is that the gap would have to be filled in some other way.[35]

Senior police officers in Britain have been less circumspect, and have stated firmly that they cannot envisage the 1992 process without their being given greatly increased powers to check for the presence of terrorists and other 'undesirables'. This conviction was expressed very clearly by the Metropolitan Police Special Branch in a memorandum to the same House of Lords inquiry.[36] While strongly opposing the whole idea of abolishing internal border controls where Britain is concerned, the memorandum goes on to lay down a set of compensatory measures which the Special Branch feels to be essential if the move towards abolition proves unstoppable. These include 'a significant increase in our surveillance capability' and a radical 'easing' of extradition arrangements between states. The memorandum also states:

> There could well be strong pressure for the introduction of some form of national identity card, extra police powers of 'stop and search', enhanced anti-terrorist legislation and more stringent registration of non-EEC nationals.

Similar views were expressed to the inquiry by the Association of Chief Police Officers (ACPO). We have been warned.

As we have seen, the British Government has so far denied that Britain's border controls must in fact be abolished to comply with the Single European Act, though the legality of this position has been questioned (see also Chapter Four). Ministers have declined to speculate on what measures they would support if Britain's virtually isolated position on this issue became untenable. However, as noted in Chapter Two the former Home Secretary has remarked: 'We certainly would not quarrel with member states ...if they wish to operate their checks on non-EC nationals in their cities or workplaces.'[37] Mr Hurd did not elaborate on how such checks could be confined to non-EC nationals, or what means might be employed for carrying them out.

For the time being, therefore, planning in Britain proceeds as if virtually nothing is going to change with regard to border controls; after 1992 there will, as at present, be a 'streamlined channel' for EC citizens entering the UK but they will still have to present their passports and be subject to spot checks (see Chapter Two). Users of the Channel Tunnel will have their passports checked on the train.[38] The danger of this somewhat complacent approach is that in the meantime it stifles debate on possible changes which may in the end be introduced in great haste, with little or no opportunity to consider the full implications.

Identity cards in Western Europe

Liberty has recently surveyed the position of a range of countries across the world regarding identity cards.[39] In Western Europe (defined as the 21 larger Council of Europe states, not counting Liechtenstein and San Marino) there are compulsory schemes in nine countries, voluntary schemes in six and no cards in six (see box overleaf). For the twelve EC countries the count is five compulsory, three voluntary and four with no scheme. Where compulsory systems do exist there are wide variations in the strictness with which they are applied, and public attitudes vary accordingly. In West Germany the system is heavily used by the police, whereas in Iceland there is no requirement to carry a card. In many cases the cards can be used instead of passports to travel to other parts of Europe.

Identity cards in Western Europe

(† indicates EC country)

Compulsory
Belgium†, Cyprus, W. Germany†, Greece†, Iceland, Luxembourg†, Malta, Spain†, Turkey.

Voluntary
Austria, Finland, France†, Italy†, Portugal†, Switzerland.

No cards
Denmark†, Ireland†, Netherlands†, Norway, Sweden, UK†.

Looking at each EC country in turn, there are no proposals to introduce identity cards in *Denmark* and human rights workers there say that there would probably be strong opposition to the idea. In the *Netherlands* the government has floated the idea of identity cards; this appears to be aimed at the allegedly large number of illegal immigrants, following pressure from other signatories of the 1985 Schengen Agreement (see Chapter Two). There is broad public opposition to their introduction in the Netherlands, and the government has insisted that if this did happen the police would have the power to demand a card only where there had been an incident to justify it. No firm proposals have yet been made.

In *France* an identity card is optional but some such proof of identity is needed in order to vote. Since 1981 the police have had the right to demand proof of identity under specified circumstances such as an immediate threat to security. In 1986 the law was changed to increase these powers and there is some disquiet about the way they are used; the police are accused of harassing young and/or non-white people on the pretext of suspected crime (e.g. in the Métro). Identity cards are not at present kept up to date regarding details such as the person's address, but there is a trial scheme to change over to machine-readable cards for which the information could be updated. There are fears that such cards could be used improperly to encode details such as political affiliation.

In *Belgium* identity cards are compulsory and everyone is supposed to carry one at all times; it is claimed by human rights workers that black people are more liable to be stopped on suspicion of being illegal immigrants. Failure to show an identity card or a passport can lead to administrative detention for up to 24 hours. Similar rules apply in *Luxembourg, Portugal* and *Spain*. In Spain there are discussions about introducing machine-readable cards, but the governing party is divided on the issue. The Spanish system is said to be disliked by young people, who feel that the police abuse it.

In *West Germany* the earlier identity books are being replaced (on renewal) by machine-readable cards issued to everyone aged over 16. There are fears that this will increase the extent of state surveillance; it is already the case that people on the way to a demonstration have been stopped and their identity card numbers noted. The police can ask for cards at any time and can detain a person without one until it is fetched.

Greece has had a compulsory system for some time but until recently the cards were issued only by a person's local police station and the system appears not to have been abused. In November 1987 a new law came into effect which introduced a national computer-linked scheme, and strong fears were expressed that this would lead to more details about a person being recorded than were needed for simple identification. A similar debate has gone on in *Italy* where there is a locally-based scheme; at present, alternative proof of identity is accepted when a card is requested (e.g. following an accident). *Ireland* has no plans for identity cards.

In *Turkey* (which hopes to join the EC) every person must carry (and show to the police when asked) a card which also lists the holder's religion and next of kin. It is alleged that the cards of ex-political prisoners are punched with holes so as to make them recognisable to the police. Those Kurds whose religion is neither Muslim nor Christian also complain that they are harassed when their cards reveal this fact.

The situation thus varies widely between countries. A universal scheme for the EC, with associated laws requiring the production of a card on demand, would therefore be likely to meet opposition in a number of countries.

Identity cards in Britain

The experience of Britain's wartime identity card is illuminating in considering the likely effect of a compulsory card system. The national registration card was introduced along with other emergency measures at the beginning of the 1939-45 war. It continued in use after the war, officially as an aid to administering the rationing system, and the same identification numbers were used for the first National Health Service medical cards. However, cards also had to be produced in connection with Post Office transactions and were often requested by the police. As one writer recalls:

> ...the police, who had by now got used to the exhilarating new belief that they could get anyone's name and address for the asking, went on calling for their production with increasing frequency. If you picked up a fountain pen in the street and handed it to a constable, he would ask to see your identity card in order that he might record your name as

> that of an honest citizen. You seldom carried it; and this meant that he had to give you a little pencilled slip requiring you to produce it at a police station within two days.[40]

The system was finally abolished in 1952 after a test case was brought.[41] This arose from the refusal of a rebellious motorist either to show his identity card to a policeman, or to accept the note requiring its later production. Although the High Court accepted that the constable was within the law, Lord Chief Justice Goddard remarked:

> Because the police may have powers, it does not follow that they ought to exercise them on all occasions ...it is obvious that the police now, as a matter of routine, demand the production of national registration cards whenever they stop or interrogate a motorist for whatever cause ...such action tends to make the people resentful of the acts of the police, and incline them to obstruct the police instead of assisting them.[41]

In recent years there have been periodic calls (unrelated to 1992) for national identity cards to be reintroduced in Britain. The Home Secretary announced in July 1988 that he was asking chief constables for their views. In November 1988 a committee of ACPO announced that it could see 'no disadvantages in principle or in practice' in having a national scheme.[42] In addition a number of more limited schemes have been suggested, including a compulsory one for football supporters (see below) and various voluntary schemes for young drinkers.[39]

Proponents of a comprehensive national system claim that identity cards would help in combating a wide range of social evils. In 1988 the Conservative MP Tony Favell attempted unsuccessfully to bring in a Bill to set up such a system; he claimed that it would control football hooliganism and 'help in the fight against terrorism and crime in general'.[43] He also suggested that it would deter 'crooks and thugs worming their way into old people's homes, often posing as gas men, meter readers or council officials'. Other MPs took up the theme: Ian Bruce claimed that identity cards would 'help a great deal in registering everybody for the community charge and in all sorts of ways, such as fighting benefit and other kinds of fraud'.[44]

In February 1989 the arguments were rehearsed again when Ralph Howell MP introduced a National Identity Card Bill.[45] The Government expressed opposition to a compulsory scheme of this kind and the Bill failed to proceed further. During the debate the Home Office junior minister, John Patten, said, 'I am aware of no evidence to suggest that identity cards have been of substantial benefit in tackling crime.'[46] However, he added: 'As we can all appreciate, immigration control at the point of entry presents particular problems to countries with land frontiers. In such countries there is a clear argument for the maintenance of some form of fairly vigorous internal control, in which I freely admit that an identity card system could play an important part.'[46] It is clear what could follow if Britain had to fall into line over internal border controls.

Civil liberty issues

It is often pointed out that the average citizen already uses a wide range of identification documents for special purposes: driving licence, passport, bank and credit cards, travel passes and so on. What difference would one more make? How do existing systems differ from a compulsory national scheme?

The common feature of the cards we commonly carry about with us is that we have chosen to apply for them in order to obtain a particular benefit or service. A passport is acquired voluntarily and is only needed (at least in theory) when crossing national borders. The nearest we have to an identity document issued to everyone is the new National Insurance Card (see also below), but this is used only when changing jobs or claiming benefit. The inconvenience of having to carry a particular card is in most cases offset by the knowledge that it gives the holder some protection against abuse of the relevant benefit by others – driving by those who are a potential danger on the road, fraudulent use of cheques, and so on. In some cases the card simply shows that the person has made a prepayment, as for a season ticket.

In special circumstances some sort of document may be demanded to prove a person's identity, for instance when sitting for an examination. In Scotland a potential witness to a crime may be required to give the police his or her name and address. However, the police and government officials have no general power (except under immigration legislation and in Northern Ireland under the Emergency Provisions Act) to stop people and ask their identity. Occasions where the police have done this extensively are of doubtful legality: examples are the checks on people travelling towards Stonehenge in summer 1985 and 1986[47] and the checks made at road blocks during the 1986 Wapping dispute.[48] A driving licence should only be demanded in Great Britain if a person is driving on a road, or (if not driving) is believed to have committed a driving offence.

In contrast, in order to serve the ends suggested for it, a compulsory identity card would have to be linked with a police power to demand it at any time and to detain those not carrying it. Penalties would need to be laid down for non-compliance. The experience of other European countries points to an obvious danger: that minorities and dissident groups are liable to be more harassed by the police when a compulsory card system is in force. We have already noted complaints on this score in Belgium, France, West Germany, Spain and Turkey. The use of card checks to identify anti-government demonstrators (as in West Germany) poses a further risk: that such people can later be monitored and discriminated against in various ways, once their numbers are recorded on a central computer. It would clearly be unwise to rely on the police never to misuse a sweeping new power to demand proof of identity.

As noted in Chapter Two, it is already the case that some groups of the British population are subject to frequent 'stop and search' procedures[49] and 'passport raids' for alleged 'overstayers' and 'illegal entrants'.[50] A number of those who gave evidence to the House of Lords inquiry into border controls were sure that identity cards would only make this worse; the representative of the United Kingdom Immigrants Advisory Service said: 'We think that it *would* have the effect of increasing the sense of insecurity among black and Asian people settled in this country or visiting this country for temporary purposes.'[51] The alternative view – that identity cards would enable black people to avoid unnecessary detention as illegal immigrants by immediately showing their cards – seems to command only minority support. The experience of police harassment by numbers of black people suggests that they would be asked to produce their identity cards disproportionately more than other groups.

The objections to identity cards are therefore very serious, and cannot be dismissed as a mere British eccentricity. A sophisticated computer-linked scheme would be so attractive to various agencies of government that once it was set up it would be almost impossible to dismantle. Furthermore, there would be no shortage of ideas on how to extend its use. The situation in Malaysia is of interest here. Under a system first set up under British rule, Malaysia now has identity cards of four different colours – blue for citizens, red for permanent residents, green for limited-stay residents and brown for ex-convicts and 'political offenders'. The colour of the card determines a person's freedom to travel, own property, obtain certain jobs, and gain access to education and social services.

The suspicion persists that, despite the firm statements of ministers (including Margaret Thatcher) which appear to accept the civil liberty arguments, the Government might be only too happy to accept an identity card system if the blame could be placed squarely on the shoulders of the bureaucrats in Brussels. Certainly the police would not complain. An indication of the Government's underlying philosophy surfaced in the parliamentary debates on the Football Spectators Bill. This incorporated an identity card scheme which was only dropped (though it remains in the 1989 Act) after devastating criticism in Lord Justice Taylor's report on the Hillsborough Stadium football disaster.[52] During earlier debates in the House of Lords the Government resisted amendments that would have limited the power of the police (or anyone else) to demand the production of identity cards away from football grounds. The Government also refused to incorporate any limits on the information that could be stored on the cards. A scheme without such limitations might have been a convenient testing ground for a much wider system.

Computers, data protection and identity cards

The trend in all countries has been to link the various plastic cards issued to individuals with central data banks, using a machine-readable printed code or a magnetic strip on the card; the cash cards issued by banks are an obvious example. Further developments involving 'smart cards' are expected soon; these are cards carrying a memory which can be modified by interaction with a terminal.

Even with a simple magnetic strip the information on a card can be added to or changed whenever it is passed through a terminal. The implications of these changes, particularly when applied to identity cards, are worrying civil rights organisations in many countries. What started out as a piece of paper carrying only essential personal details can now be transformed into a coded police dossier, labelling its unwitting carrier in ways unbeknownst to them. Only in some countries can the holder check what is on the card and even then the process is expensive: in Britain the Data Protection Act allows a charge of up to £10 for each disclosure.

The British Government has been an enthusiastic proponent of machine-readable identity documents. The new-style National Insurance Card (issued to all new holders since 1984) carries a magnetic strip capable of holding 200 characters, which has led to questions about why such a high capacity is needed. The British version of the EC passport includes machine-readable printed characters, which the Passport Office insists will convey no more than the details printed on the older type of passport. The inclusion of the machine-readable section was an option insisted on by the British Government when the recommendations for the format were being drawn up; no other European country except West Germany has so far considered it.

The debate about machine-readable documents should not, however, distract attention from the central issue: that once a universal system of identifying numbers has been established, and once the police and other officials have been given the right to demand production of this number, then further secret information can be accessed simply by feeding the number into a computer terminal. Britain, like all other European countries, now has a national police computer, and there are about 800 computer terminals in police stations across the country.[53] The UK's new and more powerful PNC2, replacing the old police national computer, is costing £13 million to instal over a period of three years.[54]

Since 1987 there has also been a growing data bank of information held by the immigration service about people suspected of evading immigration controls; it uses the same HOLMES (Home Office Large Major Enquiry System) computer system that is used by the police to make connections between many small items of information.[55]

Any complacency about the safeguards in a peaceful democratic state like Britain should be shaken by a recent scandal in Switzerland, where it emerged that the federal police held secret files on 900,000 people (about one in seven of the population).[56] The situation was repeated at local levels of government, with 75,000 such files in the Zurich canton alone.[57]

Finally, the use of computer data banks by many government agencies raises the issue (see also above) of how much *exchange* of information should be permitted. The convention that personal data collected by one agency should not be freely passed on to others, which according to one writer is 'consistently broken', is in any case being eroded by new legislation.[58] The poll tax system depends on information from a number of sources being used to ensure collection of the tax, and in fact the Local Government Finance Act 1988 specifically allows such exchanges in the case of the poll tax.[59]

It is worth quoting what Britain's Data Protection Registrar had to say at the time of the debate on the Howell Bill mentioned above:

> The act of presenting a national identity card offers the opportunity not only to determine that this individual may be who he says he is but to record information about him. This opportunity is enhanced if, as seems likely, the card is designed to be machine-readable. Any information on the card can be recorded, together with information on the whereabouts of the individual and the circumstances in which the card is used.
>
> In order to administer and control the issue of national identity cards, it would seem necessary to form a population register which could record the movement, from address to address, of all the individuals in the United Kingdom.
>
> The allotment of a National Identity Number to each citizen would open up the possibility of linking collections of information about individuals which have been obtained and are used for many diverse purposes. Through this 'data matching' it would be possible to build up a picture of an individual's life and characteristics from many disparate pieces of information.[60]

The Registrar went on to discuss the arguments for and against such developments, with examples drawn from other countries. He concluded:

> The introduction of national identity cards and national identity numbers would mark a significant step along the path to the comprehensive

recording and automatic processing of information about individuals. It is a step with potentially serious privacy implications for all United Kingdom citizens. From a privacy and data protection viewpoint the arguments suggest that the step should not be taken.[60]

Alternative schemes

Although the Government opposed the compulsory identity card proposed in the Howell Bill, ministers did not rule out the idea of a voluntary scheme if it could be made self-financing.[44] The House of Commons Home Affairs Committee had already suggested that the back page of the new EC-style passport could be issued separately as a Community travel document.[61] However, the Data Protection Registrar has warned that a 'voluntary' scheme can easily develop into a *de facto* compulsory one; an obvious example is the cheque card, which began as a voluntary back-up to the cheque book and is now effectively mandatory.[60] This point was also illustrated in the debate on the Howell Bill, when the Bill's sponsor mentioned that even the French ambassador insisted that the voluntary French identity card was compulsory.[62] This was corrected later in the debate by Home Office minister John Patten.[63]

The case for a voluntary card depends on the use for which it is intended. If it is needed only by travellers from one country to another – in case of random checks at borders, for instance – then the present EC-style passport would be perfectly adequate; such documents will continue to be valid after 1992. The Northern Ireland border is policed by inspecting driving licences or requiring people to give their names and addresses; a number of those who gave evidence to the House of Lords inquiry suggested that this ought to be sufficient for the rest of Europe.

The assertion that identity cards will be essential after 1992 for detecting terrorists and other law-breakers is unproven, particularly when one sees that the Scandinavian countries of the Nordic Union allow free travel without such a system. Professional criminals will always find a way of forging whatever document is required, and in any case it is hard to see how a system relying on frequent identity checks can fail to be oppressive to most people. The onus should be on those who propose identity cards to show how they would benefit society as a whole; the liberty of the individual should not be curtailed unless it is necessary for the preservation of the liberty of others. There is scant evidence that an identity card system would satisfy this condition.

Conclusions

Information technology is a Pandora's box of possibilities, many of them unforeseen only a few years ago: exciting for users of the new techniques, but potentially dangerous to individuals who constitute the source of the ever-increasing pool of 'name-linked data' – particularly the so-called 'sensitive data' relating to racial origin, political opinions and sexual life. For agencies of the state there is a particular temptation to exercise closer control over ordinary citizens through the storage of such information.

1992 highlights the risks involved for two reasons. Firstly, there may be a growth in internal surveillance with the proposed withering away of intra-Community frontiers. Secondly, 1992 will accelerate the existing trend towards cross-border exchanges of information; the individual's personal details will potentially be available throughout the Community.

At the same time, the philosophy behind the Single European Act offers a possible solution: to create new frameworks at Community level for the regulation of data transfers and the protection of the individual. Such frameworks, backed by the force of Community law, would be more effective than any voluntary system modelled on the Council of Europe's Convention on the subject. At present, however, there are only proposals under discussion. Some action is urgently needed.

Notes

1. See, for example, Duncan Campbell and Steve Connor, *On the Record: Surveillance, Computers and Privacy* (Michael Joseph, 1986). These authors estimated that by the year 2000, public sector data banks in Britain will probably store more than one hundred thousand million words of personal information covering the entire population, accessible from one hundred thousand computer terminals (p. 36).
2. *Official Journal of the European Communities*, L 246 (29 August 1981), p 31.
3. *Privacy Laws & Business*, April 1990, pp. 2-6 and 34-5.
4. *Ibid.*, September 1989, pp. 11 and 18.
5. *Guidelines on the Protection of Privacy and Transborder Flows of Personal Data* (Organisation for Economic Co-operation and Development, Paris, 1980).
6. *Privacy Laws & Business*, December 1989, pp. 7-12.
7. *Declaration by the Ministers Concerned with Immigration*, WGI 513 (December 1989); copy deposited with Parliament.
8. *Privacy Laws & Business*, December 1989, pp. 7-12.
9. *Ibid.*, February 1989, pp. 31-2.
10. Mark Hollingsworth and Charles Tremayne, *The Economic League: the Silent McCarthyism* (National Council for Civil Liberties, 1989).
11. *Your Right to See Your File*, Briefing No. 8 (National Council for Civil Liberties, 1987).

12. *Hansard*, 2 February 1988, col. 527.
13. *Fifth Report of the Data Protection Registrar* (HMSO, 1989), p. 9.
14. Quoted by Richard Norton-Taylor, 'Blinded by the light of technology', in *The Guardian*, 6 June 1990.
15. Report by the Secretariat for the 4th meeting of the Legal Observatory for the Information Market, Luxembourg, 14 May 1987, p. 9.
16. *Privacy Laws & Business*, February 1989, p. 4.
17. Warren Freedman, *The Right of Privacy in the Computer Age* (Quorum, 1987), p. 107.
18. *New Technologies: a Challenge to Privacy Protection?* (Council of Europe, 1989), pp. 6-8.
19. *Ibid.*, p. 15.
20. *Privacy Laws & Business*, December 1989, pp. 19-24.
21. *Who's Watching You? Video Surveillance in Public Places*, Briefing No. 16 (National Council for Civil Liberties, 1989).
22. *New Technologies: a Challenge to Privacy Protection?* (Council of Europe, 1989), p. 24.
23. *Ibid.*, p. 11.
24. For a survey of the first six Recommendations see *Privacy Laws & Business*, February 1989, pp. 17-21. For R (89) 14 see *ibid.*, December 1989, pp. 2-3.
25. *Regulating the Use of Personal Data in the Police Sector*, Recommendation R (87) 15 and Explanatory Memorandum (Council of Europe, 1988).
26. Ministers of the Trevi Group, *Programme of Action Relating to the Reinforcement of Police Co-operation and of the Endeavours to Combat Terrorism or Other Forms of Organised Crime*, June 1990; see House of Commons Home Affairs Committee, *Practical Police Co-operation in the European Community*, Session 1989-90, 7th Report, Vol. I (HMSO, 1990), pp. l-liv.
27. *Association of Chief Police Officers Code of Practice for Police Computer Systems* (ACPO, London, December 1987). Also reproduced by permission in *Encyclopaedia of Data Protection*, edited by S. N. L. Chalton and S. J. Gaskill (Sweet and Maxwell, 1988), Part 5 (Codes of Practice), sections 5-250 to 5-292, pp. 5157-84.
28. *Ibid.*, section 5-260, p. 5163.
29. House of Commons Home Affairs Committee, *Criminal Records*, Session 1989-90, 3rd Report (HMSO, 1990), p. ix.
30. *Ibid.*, p. viii.

31. Home Office statistics, quoted in *Submission to the Employment Committee on Employers' Recruitment Practices (Pre-Employment Vetting)* (National Council for Civil Liberties, 1990), Summary para. 3.0.
32. *New Technologies: a Challenge to Privacy Protection?* (Council of Europe, 1989), p. 40.
33. *Privacy Laws & Business*, December 1989, p. 1.
34. House of Lords Select Committee on the European Communities, *1992: Border Controls of People*, Session 1988-89, 22nd Report (HMSO, 1989).
35. *Ibid.*, Evidence p. 12.
36. *Ibid.*, Evidence pp. 170-3.
37. *Hansard*, 4 May 1989, col. 398.
38. *Ibid.*, 21 February 1990, cols 770w and 814w. The second written answer appears to supersede the first regarding trains terminating in London.
39. *Identity Cards and the Threat to Civil Liberties*, Briefing No. 12 (National Council for Civil Liberties, 1989).
40. C. H. Rolph, *Personal Identity* (Michael Joseph, 1957), pp. 22-3.
41. *Willcock* v. *Muckle* (1951) 49 LGR 584.
42. *The Independent*, 24 November 1988.
43. *Hansard*, 21 June 1988, col. 976.
44. *Ibid.*, 21 July 1988, col. 1262.
45. *Ibid.*, 10 February 1989, cols 1267-333.
46. *Ibid.*, 10 February 1989, col. 1303.
47. *Stonehenge: a Report into the Civil Liberties Implications of the Events Relating to the Convoys of Summer 1985 and 1986* (National Council for Civil Liberties, 1986).
48. *No Way in Wapping: the Effect of the Policing of the News International Dispute on Wapping Residents* (National Council for Civil Liberties, 1986).
49. David J. Smith and Jeremy Grey, *Police and People in London* (Gower, 1985).
50. Paul Gordon, *Policing Immigration: Britain's Internal Controls* (Pluto, 1985), pp. 23-6 and 51-7.
51. House of Lords Select Committee on the European Communities, *1992: Border Controls of People*, Session 1988-89, 22nd Report (HMSO, 1989), Evidence p. 55.
52. *The Hillsborough Stadium Disaster – Final Report*, Cm. 962 (HMSO, 1990).
53. Richard Norton-Taylor, *In Defence of the Realm? The Case for Accountable Security Services* (Civil Liberties Trust, 1990), pp. 66-7.
54. House of Commons Home Affairs Committee, *Criminal Records*, Session 1989-90, 3rd Report (HMSO, 1990), pp. 17-21.

55. Jolyon Jenkins, 'Foreign exchange', in *New Statesman & Society*, 28 July 1989, pp. 12-13.
56. *Financial Times*, 7 March 1990.
57. *Tages-Anzeiger* (Zurich), 1 December 1989.
58. Richard Norton-Taylor, *In Defence of the Realm? The Case for Accountable Security Services* (Civil Liberties Trust, 1990), p. 65.
59. *Privacy & the Poll Tax: A Guide to Good Practice for Local Government Officers* (National Council for Civil Liberties, 1989).
60. *Fifth Report of the Data Protection Registrar* (HMSO, 1989), Appendix AA3.
61. House of Commons Home Affairs Committee, *Previous Recommendations*, Session 1987-88, 5th Report (HMSO, 1988). See also the Committee's recent report, *Practical Police Co-operation in the European Community*, Session 1989-90, 7th Report, Vol. I (HMSO, 1990), paras 127-38.
62. *Hansard*, 21 July 1988, col. 1274.
63. *Ibid*., col. 1303.

CHAPTER FOUR

Policing Europe

The Treaty of Rome and the Single European Act are silent on two problems highlighted by the 1992 process: the wide variations between European police forces in their organisation and methods, and the differences between systems of criminal justice in the EC states. The prospect of freedom of movement for people in breach of the law, as well as for those who are not, has led police spokesmen in a number of countries to express alarm, and new questions have arisen in a range of areas: 'hot pursuit' across borders, exchanges of information between police forces (see Chapter Three), and even the possibility of some kind of 'Europolice' with Community-wide powers. All these questions raise urgent issues of accountability. In the realm of cross-border co-operation between judicial authorities, existing disagreements between governments over such matters as extradition have been sharpened by the approach of 1992.

Differing traditions within Europe

Britain's legal system (Scotland aside) is unique in Europe in being based on common law and the extensive use of oral evidence, though this was modified by the Police and Criminal Evidence Act 1984. Continental states rely more on written constitutions and written depositions; there are also major differences in judicial procedure. Britain has an adversarial system of settling the question of guilt by a contest between lawyers in the courtroom, rather than relying (as in France, for instance) on an examining magistrate (trained as a judge) to investigate this before the trial.

The organisation of police forces is even more diverse.[1] The UK has 52 locally-based police forces (not counting specialist forces like the British Transport Police). West Germany is comparable with Britain in having separate police forces in the 11 *Länder* (the component states of the Federal Republic), but there is also a Federal criminal investigation agency, the *Bundeskriminalamt* or BKA. France has three kinds of police force: municipal police, national police and the gendarmerie. Belgium is said to have no less than 68 such organisations, though some of these cover offences which in other countries are civil rather than criminal matters.[2]

Control of the police follows differing patterns as well. In France, for instance, the municipal police (who have only limited powers) are answerable to the local mayor; the national police, who cover all towns with more than 10,000 inhabitants, answer to the Minister of the Interior; and the paramilitary gendarmerie (which covers the rest of the country) is controlled by the Minister of Defence. In each area, however, overall responsibility for policing rests not with a police officer but with a government-appointed prefect who is a civilian. While there are many reservations about the French system, the intense rivalry between the two major police forces tends indirectly to help maintain accountability, because each monitors the other closely for any malpractice. In Britain, the strong group loyalty between police forces in the face of criticism rather detracts from public confidence in their accountability.

The Council of Europe has been working for many years on proposals for harmonising and simplifying the legal procedures of criminal justice across Europe, and has drawn up a number of Conventions, Resolutions and Recommendations in this field; examples are the 1957 European Convention on Extradition (see below) and the influential Recommendation R (87) 15 on the use of personal data by the police (see Chapter Three).[3] The European Commission has dealt with harmonising those laws and regulations that are relevant to the achievement of the internal market. However, neither of these bodies has tackled the wide variations between countries in the practical organisation of policing and criminal investigation. The problems of achieving harmonisation appear almost insuperable, and on many issues the member states have not even tried. What is happening instead is an *ad hoc* increase in co-operation between police forces, sometimes driven (as in the case of the Channel Tunnel) by the obvious need to sort out the division of responsibility. There is thus no master plan nor any prospect of one. Nevertheless, some changes have already been made or are being proposed, and these require careful examination from the civil liberty point of view. We consider first the question of policing, and then discuss the changes made to laws relating to extradition and other areas of mutual assistance between countries.

Police accountability in Britain

The most relevant issue with regard to policing after 1992 is that of accountability, since any drawing together of Europe's police forces must raise the question of who is to control their collective activities. In Britain the tripartite structure established by the Police Act 1964 divides responsibility for each force outside London between the Chief Constable, the Home Secretary and a police authority comprised of two-thirds local councillors and one-third magistrates. In London the Metropolitan Police are responsible only to the Home Secretary.

The powers of local authorities are limited to appointing chief constables and their deputies (subject to Home Office approval), voting on the police budget, and ensuring the maintenance of an adequate and efficient police force. Some but not all of them have sub-committees for the consideration of complaints against the police. The tripartite system has been the subject of persistent criticism, particularly on the grounds that Parliament has no direct control; the Home Secretary can evade most questions on police activities by saying that operational matters are left to chief constables.[4] At the same time the Government has influence on the police behind the scenes; the Home Office issues official circulars on a range of topics, and the Home Secretary receives reports on each force from the government-appointed Inspectorate of Constabulary. These were formerly confidential but are now published.

The lack of parliamentary accountability is compounded by the increasing tendency for police policy to be formulated by a body which is not accountable to anyone outside the police – the Association of Chief Police Officers (ACPO). ACPO represents chief constables and their senior assistants in England, Wales and Northern Ireland, and there is a similar body ACPO(S) for Scotland. Although having no formal power to act on behalf of Britain's police, ACPO has increasingly come to influence policy through its working parties and sub-committees. One of these is the International Affairs Advisory Committee whose function is 'to oversee the police service contribution to international discussions', and the Government has encouraged the development of the ACPO secretariat 'to enable ACPO to contribute more effectively to discussions and the provision of advice affecting the service'.[5] Perhaps most importantly, members of ACPO are closely involved in the secret meetings of the Trevi group (see Chapter One) which deals (among other things) with the policing implications of 1992.

As bodies such as the Association of Metropolitan Authorities have pointed out, the main problem with this, together with the increasingly close relationship between ACPO and the Government, is that the third party in the British system of accountability – the local police authority – is effectively excluded. As a result, finance and resources allocated by police authorities may be absorbed not only for acceptable ends like combating terrorism, but also for more contentious projects in areas such as immigration control or information exchange.[6]

Cross-border policing

The dissolving of internal frontiers draws attention to a growing problem that police forces have been aware of for some time: the international character of terrorism and some categories of serious crime. Since 1979 there have been informal meetings between EC police officers twice a year. The purpose of these meetings is 'the exchange of operational information on terrorism and serious crime'.[7]

'Hot pursuit' has now been agreed (within limits) by the partners in the Schengen Convention (see Chapter Two), and will undoubtedly be advocated as a model for adoption by the rest of the Community. The Trevi Group of

EC interior ministers, which deals with terrorism and drug trafficking, has so far decided only to '...examine the principle of, and conditions under which, authorisation might be granted, for States that so wish, notably by means of bilateral agreements, for the crossing of common land frontiers by our respective agencies...'[8]

Existing agreements of this sort are confined to the Scandinavian countries and the Benelux group.[2] The issue of policemen even entering another country in search of evidence has been fraught with diplomatic difficulties, and in Britain the Home Office has issued a circular warning of the need to seek permission through official channels in every case.[9]

In the popular imagination, no doubt fostered by radio and television series, sophisticated co-operation exists between police forces through Interpol (the International Criminal Police Organisation), leading to the relentless pursuit of criminals around the world. The reality is more mundane; under its constitution Interpol has no powers of investigation or pursuit, being no more than a clearing house for information and a forum for discussion.[10] Each of the 146 member countries has a National Central Bureau to handle information (Britain's is housed by New Scotland Yard). Interpol's power is limited to the 'red notice' – a request for the arrest of a suspect with the assurance that an extradition request will follow. Interpol is not seen by most police officers and academic specialists as a useful vehicle for integrating the European police forces.

There is, in fact, disagreement over whether 1992 will actually make much difference to policing issues; some see Europe being swamped by uncontrollable crime, while others point out that many European borders are already effectively open, so that no great change is to be expected. This lack of agreement is accompanied by a corresponding lack of clear ideas on what exactly might be done. At a police conference in 1989 the director of the Netherlands Police Academy pointed out the underlying difficulty, namely the complete absence of research on the consequences that open borders will have for the police: '...the police have just started to think about the problem and the best they have are some general ideas about possible consequences over which they disagree amongst themselves.'[2]

There is also some disagreement between the police and customs officials. In the UK, bodies such as ACPO have stated their formal opposition to the idea of abolishing border controls, but have also indicated that in the event of this happening they would expect to be given extra powers and resources (see Chapter Two). The UK Customs and Excise service resists the whole idea of dismantling frontiers and offers no alternative, quoting Margaret Thatcher as saying: '...it is a matter of plain common sense that we cannot totally abolish frontier controls...' and pointing to the large proportion of drugs seized at the borders of the UK compared with seizures inland.[11]

As we have seen in Chapter Two, the Government's intention appears to be to maintain after 1992 the current system under which there is a 'fast lane' for the entry of EC citizens into Britain, with spot checks by immigration, customs or Special Branch officers. The police have complained that this system was introduced without consulting them, and that it 'leaves little opportunity for identifying persons involved in terrorism, or otherwise of interest to police'.[12] However, even such spot checks might be ruled inconsistent with the Single European Act (SEA). According to one writer, the British position may prove to be untenable:

> The Commission's view is that the SEA is quite explicit, namely that any derogation from the principle must be temporary and must cause the least possible disturbance to the fulfilment of the aim of free movement. Therefore a citizen of the EC may take the British Government to the European Court [of Justice] for failure to carry out its obligations if passage is 'unnecessarily' impeded.[13]

It is possible that the European Commission will not press the issue; the Commission itself is vulnerable to the criticism that it makes sweeping statements about the ineffectiveness of frontier checks on the basis of very little research.[14] However, in order to hasten the process of abolishing frontiers, Commission President Jacques Delors suggested to the Rhodes summit in December 1988 that each country should appoint a co-ordinator with responsibility for speeding up the resolution of border problems between countries.[7] The result was the Co-ordinators' Group which produced the Palma Document (Chapters One and Two).

From the civil liberty point of view, the lack of so much basic information points to a further risk in the 1992 process: that if border checks are abolished throughout the Community, there is a danger that extra measures for strengthening internal controls will be rushed through as a result of some unexpected crisis – perhaps a new wave of European terrorism, or an alarming increase in drug trafficking – to the detriment of civil liberties which are diminished through lack of proper consideration. We have already noted that such measures would be likely to bear most heavily on certain sections of the population, particularly black and ethnic minority people.

Reorganising the police

We have seen that Britain is not alone among EC countries in having more than one police force, but the lack of ultimate control over many of their actions by both central government and local authorities appears to be unique; it reflects the basic inadequacy of the British system. Douglas Hurd, former Home Secretary, told an ACPO conference:

> At international debates on policing issues, I have to explain that, although I am the minister responsible for the police service, I am unable to make commitments on operational decisions. That causes considerable surprise. Surprise turns to incredulity when our foreign partners learn that even the representatives of chief officers are unable to deliver binding commitments on behalf of their colleagues.[15]

Hurd went on to encourage ACPO to become more of a representative and policy-determining body – a role which, as we have seen, ACPO has actively developed. He seemed unconcerned about the issue of accountability, quoting only the principle that where operational judgements are concerned, every chief officer is accountable to the law and therefore to the courts.

Whatever the role of ACPO, the multiplicity of forces in Britain is regarded as a problem by some sections of the police because of imperfect communications between them, and the question of integration into larger groupings has become a live issue. On this point the smaller and less powerful forces are more fearful than the larger ones, which can more readily see themselves operating at a European level.

In addressing ACPO, Douglas Hurd hastened to add that he was not in favour of an all-powerful Minister of the Interior; nor did he advocate a national police force or regional forces. What he did suggest was a national criminal intelligence office to cover all forms of crime.[15] The following year (1990), in evidence to a House of Commons Select Committee, Home Secretary David Waddington also rejected the idea of a national police force or a British FBI, but said he saw a strong case for establishing a national criminal intelligence unit to deal with organised crime.[16]

Plans for such a unit had, in fact, already been announced at the 1990 ACPO conference, with the expectation that it would start to function in the summer or autumn of 1991. Soon afterwards it was announced that the new unit would also incorporate the present regional crime squads, as well as expanding the work of the national intelligence units for drugs and football hooliganism.[17] This will raise the same issues of accountability and control as a new FBI-type body, though John Dellow (the president of ACPO) is reported as saying that it will give 'the same benefits without legislation and without upsetting chief constables unhappy about a national force'.[17]

This scheme bears a strong resemblance to that suggested in 1989 by Sir Peter Imbert, the head of the Metropolitan Police.[18] At the time, there was reported to be opposition to the idea within the ACPO working party set up to study the matter,[19] and the chairman of the Police Federation had expressed polite dissent: '...our view is that anything that increases the power of the centre at the expense of the rest of the service is undesirable'.[20]

The possibility of some kind of European police force is also very controversial. In Britain the idea has been aired by a former Chief Constable, John Alderson, who wrote in July 1988: 'It may be that in due course some police organisation of a federal nature may require to be developed to deal with the most serious crimes as problems change or intensify.'[21] Alderson suggested that the European Commission could develop a Community-wide police function of the kind exercised by its existing fisheries inspectorate – though this is entitled only to be present at inspections and monitoring operations carried out by the national inspectorate concerned.

In 1989, Roger Birch (the chairman of ACPO's International Affairs Advisory Committee) dismissed such suggestions as premature; after discussing the legal difficulties, he said: 'I do not think that by 1992 and for some years beyond, the citizens of Europe will be ready to accept police officers from another part of the Community making active enquiries within their local community.'[22] However, he did suggest later to the House of Commons Home Affairs Committee that a Police Council of Europe should be set up to accelerate co-operation between European police forces.[23]

The Government response to suggestions for a European police force has been in line with its attitude to most proposals for pan-European institutions. Home Secretary David Waddington, when also giving evidence to the Home Affairs Committee, said that neither he nor his European counterparts viewed a European police force as practical politics, given that it will be 1991 before even a European Drugs Intelligence Unit is agreed; he believed a European police force to be 'aeons away'.[24]

A more robust view has been expressed by a senior Belgian policeman, Paul van Hecke, who said: 'What we need is a Europol next to Interpol. If wishes were horses, beggars might ride. Not as a duplicate, a surrogate, but as an organisation with real executive powers throughout Europe.'[25]

Another Belgian officer, Frans Geysel, has called for a code of Community crimes covering the main forms of organised international crime and breaches of Community law, together with 'a true European police force to tackle such crimes and supranational courts to sit in judgement'.[26]

A more limited suggestion has been made by the head of West Germany's *Bundeskriminalamt* (the federal criminal investigation agency) who favours a European Criminal Police Office defined as 'a central agency with investigative responsibilities'.[27] He also said: 'Europe must change its attitudes. The formal requirements for officers of one country operating in the territory of another, for instance engaging in surveillance operations or cross-border pursuit, must be reduced to a minimum.' However, the police forces of the separate *Länder* comprising the Federal Republic are said to be much less keen on such an approach, and in France the *Gendarmerie Nationale* dislikes the idea of ceding any of its authority.

Sovereignty and legitimacy

Apart from limited agreements on 'hot pursuit' and cross-border surveillance, politicians have on the whole, as in the Schengen Convention (see Chapter Two), avoided the issue of supranational policing. Ministers have so far confined themselves to signing broad declarations on closer co-operation in training, technology, information exchange and the appointment of liaison officers; the ministers of the Trevi Group signed such an agreement in December 1989.[8] However, at a 1988 EC summit meeting Chancellor Kohl of West Germany proposed that there should be a European bureau of investigation along the lines of the FBI in the USA.[28]

There are two underlying problems: that of sovereignty, and that of legitimacy. Both are discussed by author Malcolm Anderson in his history of Interpol. On sovereignty, he remarks:

> ...the doctrine of sovereignty is still almost universally accepted in the field of criminal justice and criminal law enforcement. Liberals and socialists, democrats and authoritarians hold the view that the authoritative source of criminal law is the state and the means of its enforcement should be exclusively controlled by the state... Integrated police operations are not possible until the theory and practice of state sovereignty changes.[29]

Anderson accepts that attitudes to sovereignty are changing in Europe (though more slowly in Britain), and adds: 'Willingness to pool sovereignty depends on the seriousness of the perceived threat and the effectiveness of the proposed arrangements.'[30] However, as mentioned in Chapter One, the question of altering the constitutional framework of the Community to allow closer political union is being aired with increasing forcefulness. Although such proposals are strongly challenged by the current British government, the significance of sovereignty as a critical factor in developments like EC policing may well wane in the coming decade. On the second underlying problem of legitimacy, Anderson has this to say:

> International police co-operation confronts a difficult problem of legitimacy, analogous to the problem of legitimacy of policing within states. There is always public concern, bordering on suspicion, about the police. This is sometimes justified, because policing involves coercion, a degree of confidentiality or secrecy, and contact with criminals whose

> outlook [and] values may be contagious. Police legitimacy in the domestic context is secured by scrupulous observance of the law and by wide public support for police action. In international institutions of police co-operation there is no precise equivalent of domestic law; police officers involved in these institutions have little contact with the public affected by these activities and therefore little opportunity of building up public support. But sources of legitimacy must be found, even at one remove, through national police forces and national governments.[31]

He goes on to point out that 'uncontrolled and unaccountable police forces can produce greater insecurity and oppression than ordinary criminality... It is imprudent and unrealistic to regard the police as invariably benign...'[31] His solution is that there should be formal treaty agreements on police co-operation, stating clearly what is expected of the police officers involved; this sentiment would no doubt be echoed by those police spokesmen who have complained bitterly that they are not adequately consulted or informed by the architects of 1992. A second component of Anderson's solution is publicity for all major forms of co-operative activity: '...the ready availability of information is the only sure foundation on which to build public trust.'[32]

Civil liberty implications

How would all these proposals affect civil liberties? One danger has been referred to earlier in this chapter: that a sudden perceived threat might initiate a rapid, Community-wide integration of policing without proper safeguards. This could lead to the introduction of an unaccountable force that would subsequently be difficult to control – though if political union in the Community developed sufficiently, such a force could be subjected to scrutiny and control by the European Parliament.

Even without a new threat, the problem within Britain is that the approach of 1992 has been accompanied by the creation of national police agencies (such as drugs and football intelligence units) which are even less accountable in practice than the existing locally-based ones; now it seems likely that there will soon be a national intelligence unit for all organised crime.[17] This agency would presumably be responsible to Parliament through the Home Secretary – but as we have seen, that arrangement does not guarantee real accountability.

A second danger has already been discussed in Chapter Three: that increased police co-operation will lead to an ever-increasing exchange of information which may at present lie outside the scope of national data protection laws. The Trevi Group decided in 1986 to set up a secure communications system for exchanging intelligence on terrorism.[8] Other networks are no doubt planned or already in place for other classes of international crime.

What chance would a wrongly accused suspect have of correcting errors in such information? It is problems like this that make a strong Community agreement on enforceable data protection particularly urgent, and the new draft Directive on data protection (Chapter Three) is a step in the right direction. To be fully effective, such a Directive would also have to cover the exchange of information between security services of EC states; in Britain at least, such services – MI5, MI6, the Special Branch and the Government Communications Headquarters (GCHQ) – are totally outside democratic scrutiny.[33] There would also need to be control over the transmission of sensitive personal data.

A further problem concerning data protection is the scope for misuse of the information stored on police computers, with profound implications for personal privacy. There is already concern in Britain about the haphazard and unaccountable system of giving employers access to police records on individuals, for the purpose of pre-employment vetting (see Chapter Three). Whatever the law on data protection, the potential for misuse will dramatically increase when police data bases all over Europe are linked. It is already recognised as a problem within Britain; at a recent police conference, the police officer in charge of the User Requirements Division said:

> Misuse of information on police records has always been possible, even before computerisation. The potential for misuse increased dramatically when the first PNC [Police National Computer] application went live in 1974. As more national on-line information services become available so the potential for misuse increases.[34]

Whatever reforms are attempted, it will be vital for police forces everywhere to be made fully aware of the implications of the European Convention on Human Rights (Chapter Six). John Alderson has suggested that this should be done within the machinery of the Trevi Group, whose remit already includes police training.[35]

Harmonising legislation

Articles 18 and 19 of the Single European Act, which added Articles 100a and 100b to the Treaty of Rome, demand the progressive harmonisation of national laws 'which have as their object the establishment and functioning of the internal market'; they allow some measures to be passed without a unanimous vote (see Chapter One), though this does not apply to matters relating to the free movement of persons. No mention is made of criminal justice. However, since the dismantling of borders will give freedom of movement to everyone including people wanted by the police, the argument for closer co-operation in areas such as extradition has gained force. The Council of Europe has been encouraging moves in this direction for some time. Britain has been moving towards ratifying (in late 1990) two of the Council of Europe's Conventions: one on extradition, and another on mutual assistance in criminal matters. These are discussed below.

Extradition

This has long been an area of contention between Britain and its European partners. On the British side there have been angry outbursts at what the Government perceives to be the failure of other governments to extradite 'obviously guilty' members of the IRA, while governments on the Continent have complained of the difficulty of satisfying British courts over the evidence required. The situation so far has been complex, with a large number of separate extradition treaties operating between Britain and other countries.[36] Special arrangements operate with the Republic of Ireland under the Backing of Warrants (Republic of Ireland) Act 1965 and the Republic's largely reciprocal Extradition Act 1965.

In addition there are various international conventions on the return of those accused of aircraft hijacking, hostage-taking and so on. The 1957 European Convention on Extradition offers a common set of principles and has been ratified by many countries. Of the EC states, neither Belgium nor the UK had done so by 1990.

The stumbling-block for Britain was the fact that until recently extradition under UK law required the presentation of *prima facie* evidence acceptable to an English court (see below); in practice this applied also in Scotland, where different rules normally operate.[36] This involved the taking of oral evidence, but some countries have no provision for the taking of such evidence on oath. In addition, in some countries the evidence of witnesses is reported in writing by a police officer acting as an agent of the examining magistrate; in British courts such evidence has been treated as inadmissible hearsay evidence. In order to overcome this difficulty the Government changed the law through the Police and Criminal Evidence Act 1984 and the Criminal Justice Act 1988, in which Section 6(4) states:

> Where an Order in Council... is in force in relation to the foreign state, there is no need to furnish the court of committal with evidence sufficient to warrant the trial of the arrested person if the extradition crime had taken place within the jurisdiction of the court [i.e. within England and Wales].

This was subsequently repeated in the Extradition Act 1989, a 'consolidating measure' incorporating various earlier provisions on extradition.

The removal of the *prima facie* rule for extradition cases was strongly opposed at the time by a wide range of legal and other organisations, including the National Council for Civil Liberties; only those representing the police were in favour. It remains a source of disquiet among lawyers:

> This has been the major debating point of the [1988 Criminal Justice] Act, changing, as it does, the basic requirements of English law, and now permitting hearsay evidence and abolishing the right of the accused, if not to confront his accusers, at least to argue that the evidence is insufficient.[37]

During the passage of the legislation it was pointed out that we were giving up a fundamental safeguard for the accused with no apparent benefit in return; Britain and the Irish Republic are the only countries in Europe to allow the extradition of their own citizens (as opposed to trying them at home), and ratifying the Council of Europe's Convention (which gives countries discretion on the issue) will not change the situation. A Home Office official recently told the House of Commons Home Affairs Committee of a trend towards greater co-operation between EC countries 'to ensure that offenders do come to trial and do serve their sentences'.[38]

One may ask why the Government was prepared to abandon the *prima facie* rule so readily, when in other respects there has been no reluctance to appear an 'odd man out' in Europe. Perhaps a wish not to appear 'soft on crime' and a desire to encourage the return of IRA suspects have played some part; there was also a need to settle a long-running dispute with Spain over the extradition of criminals living there. The 1988 Home Office discussion paper on the related issue of mutual assistance in areas other than extradition has this to say:

> The United Kingdom's failure to participate in formal mutual legal assistance arrangements has earned us a poor reputation for co-operation, even in the event of entirely reasonable and proper requests. It has also caused serious problems for our own prosecution authorities as other states may refuse to render assistance because of lack of reciprocity.[39]

Despite this claim there is likely to be renewed debate when Parliament is presented with the extradition Convention before its ratification. The Government's arguments for abandoning the *prima facie* rule have been somewhat flawed throughout; for instance, it appears not to be true (as claimed) that we could not ratify the Convention while retaining the *prima facie* rule, since some countries (Norway and Israel) have done so while entering reservations regarding the evidence required. The most fundamental objection to abolition of the rule remains the one spelt out before the passing of the 1988 Act:

> To abolish the *prima facie* rule would be to establish a double standard, even between British citizens, depending on whether they were accused by foreign or domestic authorities. The British public will surely find it difficult to accept a British national being extradited to face trial abroad – with all the hardship and difficulty which accompany such an experience – on the basis of evidence which has not been submitted to a British court and would not be sufficient to commit him or her for trial should he or she be prosecuted here.[40]

The changes being planned for 1992 in no way invalidate the argument against such 'downward harmonisation'.

In addition, the Government proposes to join an agreement between EC member states for a simplified extradition system that eliminates the use of diplomatic channels for passing on requests, and also allows the facsimile transmission of documents. As yet unpublished, this agreement[41] stems from the Working Group on Judicial Co-operation set up by European Political Co-operation (see Chapter One). The Government claims that the consequent changes required in national legislation are 'useful but relatively narrow'.[42] In view of what has already happened, however, this claim may require examination for any further erosion of safeguards.

Finally, in relation to terrorism the European Parliament has urged closer co-operation in the field of extradition, and coupled this with a call for 'the creation of a European legal, police and judicial area, which is a basic precondition for the achievement of European unity'.[43]

Other mutual assistance

The Council of Europe's 1959 European Convention on Mutual Assistance in Criminal Matters was drawn up at a time when there was only limited support for the Convention on Extradition; it laid down procedures applying to lesser matters such as the examination of witnesses, experts and persons in custody, and the transmission of information from judicial records.[44] It gained new impetus with the general alarm at a perceived increase in international crime; Britain, however, held back because of the dependence of English courts on oral testimony.

With changes in the laws of evidence (see above), these difficulties were removed; the 1988 Home Office discussion paper[39] was followed by the Criminal Justice (International Co-operation) Act 1990, making it possible to ratify the Convention on Mutual Assistance. The main points regarding mutual assistance are as follows:

- service of summonses and other judicial documents relating to criminal proceedings in another country;

- service of UK summonses overseas;
- requests to overseas authorities for assistance in obtaining evidence for use in UK proceedings or investigations;
- taking of evidence in UK courts for use overseas;
- temporary transfer of convicted UK prisoners to give evidence or other assistance overseas;
- similar transfer of overseas prisoners to the UK;
- powers of search and seizure to assist investigations in other countries;
- powers to enforce overseas court orders for the forfeiture of property used in the commission of serious offences; and
- application to service courts martial.

The Act follows the main requirements of the Convention on Mutual Assistance (apart from an unrelated Part II concerning drug trafficking), and includes certain safeguards for the individual: a person whose presence is required by a foreign state as a witness or as a defendant is to be advised of the consequences of either accepting or declining the invitation, and prisoners in custody have a similar option of refusing to go.

The Act does not, however, follow the Convention in its list of circumstances in which a request for assistance may be refused. The Convention allows a government to refuse assistance to another state in the case of political or fiscal offences; it also provides for requests for search or seizure of property to be dependent on certain conditions declared by the requested state (e.g. that the relevant offence is an extraditable one in that state).

The earlier discussion paper considered the wisdom of including all these reservations in the statute, together with others drawn from a new Commonwealth scheme for mutual assistance.[39] However, it implied that these measures were unnecessary. Where fiscal offences are concerned, the Act allows assistance to be given to Commonwealth countries and those having an appropriate treaty with the UK; this is the case for all member states of the Council of Europe.

The only other grounds for refusal of assistance spelt out in the Act relate to powers of entry, search and seizure; they include a requirement that the relevant offence must be an arrestable offence in the UK, but not necessarily an extraditable one. The power to search 'is only a power to search to the extent that is reasonably required for the purpose of discovering such evidence as is there mentioned [in the warrant]'. It appears to leave open the potential for harassing people whom the police regard as 'undesirable'. A restriction to extraditable offences might have been safer, since in such cases more evidence of potential guilt would be required.

Northern Ireland

Whatever improvements are made in criminal justice co-operation within the EC, Northern Ireland will remain a potential source of dispute between the British Government and its partners because of the exceptional changes made to the judicial system there. The Diplock court system, under which certain serious offences are tried by one judge sitting without a jury, raises the question of whether a fair trial is ensured.[45] Another controversial aspect of British law is the system of exclusion orders under the Prevention of Terrorism (Temporary Provisions) Act 1989 (and earlier versions). These orders can prohibit named individuals from entering Northern Ireland, mainland Britain or both. Orders made against citizens of another EC country (e.g. the Irish Republic) could be ruled contrary to EC law because they limit freedom of movement between countries, but this has not so far been tested.[46] Such matters make international co-operation in criminal justice and other matters distinctly problematic where Northern Ireland is involved.

Extradition to Northern Ireland from the Republic of Ireland is a recurrent source of disagreement between the Irish and British governments, because of the reasons given by Irish courts for refusing to extradite IRA suspects.[47] In the 1970s the Republic's High Court tended to take the view that the alleged offences came within the definition of non-extraditable 'political offences' as generally accepted in international law. However, there has never been universal agreement on this definition. The Irish Government's position changed with the signing of the Anglo-Irish Agreement in 1985, and in 1987 the Republic passed an Act enabling it to ratify the 1977 European Convention on the Suppression of Terrorism.[48] This Convention severely restricts the grounds for pleading that an offence is 'political' and not subject to extradition.

However, disagreement with the British government erupted again in 1990 when the Irish Supreme Court refused to allow the extradition of Owen Carron on the grounds that his offence was political; the justification for this decision was that the Republic's 1987 Act applied only to offences committed after passage of the Act, and the warrant for Carron's arrest had pre-dated the Act.[49] This decision followed others in which different objections had been upheld: technical defects in the application for extradition, or the difficulty of ensuring a fair trial following public statements by British politicians, or in a recent example, the ruling that escaped IRA prisoners might face ill-treatment if returned to prison in Northern Ireland (where such cases have occurred).[50] Other countries have also shown reluctance to extradite IRA suspects to Britain.[47]

Conclusions

The fields of policing and criminal justice could turn out to be another instance of harmonisation being a one-way process, with benefits for Big Brother but potential losses for the individual. Such fears will no doubt be dismissed in terms similar to those used in discussing policing issues within the UK, where (for instance) policemen and politicians tend to justify increased surveillance by saying 'innocent people have nothing to fear' or 'what about the civil liberty to be free of crime'.

These arguments are as dangerous as they are complacent, but they remain common enough; for instance, when addressing European police chiefs, Sir Peter Imbert remarked: 'Provided basic human rights are safeguarded, we may need to recognise that laws and procedures relating to international co-operation need not be exactly the same as those applicable to internal domestic matters.'[51] The key question is how 'basic' those human rights are to be, and what justification there is for applying different standards to domestic and trans-national laws and procedures. A more public airing of the issues is therefore urgently needed.

The other vitally important consideration is that of accountability. We have already seen that there are wide variations within the EC as to how responsibility for the police is allocated. In all countries there is a need to discuss whether present systems of accountability to local communities (where they exist at all) are adequate, and whether the ordinary citizen has access to an effective system of investigating complaints against the police.

These questions apply with particular force to the UK, where there is a clear need to examine the system of accountability at both local and national levels. This is necessary in order to inform any decisions taken on supranational policing. Attention has hitherto been almost entirely focused on national and trans-national policing structures. John Alderson has echoed the fears of others that too many decisions about 1992 are being left to private meetings between the Home Office and ACPO. He calls for a much wider public debate on the implications of 1992, and says: 'If we are going to have something approaching a national police force in the future it must be really accountable.'[52]

A sign of changing attitudes among legislators is evident in the recent report on police co-operation in the EC by the House of Commons Home Affairs Committee, to which the National Council for Civil Liberties (Liberty) had submitted evidence.[53] As well as endorsing Liberty's warning of the dangers of unregulated information exchange, the report also cited Liberty's conclusion that 'what is needed... is not an *ad hoc* approach to 1992 in which ACPO and the Government sort out the problems as they think fit, but a radical rethinking of the 1964 Police Act...' The Committee said 'we entirely concur with this view', and went on to conclude as follows:

> We recommend that the Government should now publish a Consultation Document on the organisation, funding and accountability of the British police. It should seek the advice of those with policing, management, finance and civil liberties expertise, and then come forward with White Paper proposals for a police structure for Britain which will suit the needs of the twenty-first century.[54]

Notes

1. For a summary of the organisation of police forces in Belgium, Denmark, France, West Germany, Italy, Luxembourg, the Netherlands, Spain and UK, see *Policing Europe After 1992*, edited by J. C. Alderson and W. A. Tupman (Centre for Police Studies, Exeter University, 1990), pp. 6-29. For articles relating to Italy, Spain, Sweden and the UK and a discussion of European police co-operation, see *Police and Public Order in Europe*, edited by John Roach and Jurgan Thomaneck, (Croom Helm, 1985).
2. P. Van Reenen, in *Proceedings of 1989 International Police Exhibition and Conference* (Major Exhibitions and Conferences Ltd, London, 1989), Session 9, pp. 18-23; also *European Affairs*, No. 2 (1989), pp. 45-53.
3. The Council of Europe has drawn up 15 European Conventions in the field of criminal justice; they include those on extradition (1957), mutual assistance in criminal matters (1959), the punishment of road traffic offences (1964), the international validity of criminal judgments (1970), the transfer of proceedings in criminal matters (1972), the suppression of terrorism (1977), the acquisition and possession of firearms by individuals (1978), the transfer of sentenced persons (1983), and the compensation of victims of violent crime (1983). Resolutions and Recommendations cover a wide range of subjects in criminal justice, penal policy and research into crime.
4. Sarah Spencer, *Called to Account: the Case for Police Accountability in England and Wales* (National Council for Civil Liberties, 1985); *Police Accountability*, Briefing No. 3 (National Council for Civil Liberties, 1986).
5. House of Commons Home Affairs Committee, *Practical Police Co-operation in the European Community*, Session 1989-90, 7th Report, Memoranda of Evidence p. 15.
6. *Ibid.*, pp. 59-60.
7. Frans Geysels, 'Benelux, the forerunner of the European Community in the field of the free movement of persons across internal frontiers?', *Police Journal*, Vol. 63 (1990), No. 2, p. 116. This article also describes bilateral policing agreements between Belgium and neighbouring countries, and gives a detailed account of the organisation of the Trevi Group.

8. Declaration of Trevi Group Ministers, 15 December 1989 (copy deposited with Parliament).
9. *Communication with Police Forces Abroad – Amendment of Consolidated Circular*, Home Office Circular 17/1989 (17 February 1989).
10. Malcolm Anderson, *Policing the World* (Clarendon, 1989), pp. 1-11.
11. House of Lords Select Committee on the European Communities, *1992: Border Controls of People*, Session 1988-89, 22nd Report (HMSO, 1989), Evidence pp. 127-32.
12. House of Commons Home Affairs Committee, *Practical Police Co-operation in the European Community*, 7th Report, Session 1989-90 (HMSO, 1990), Memoranda of Evidence p. 21.
13. K. G. Robertson, *1992: The Security Implications* (Institute for European Defence & Strategic Studies, 1989), p. 12.
14. *Ibid.*, p. 22.
15. Home Secretary's speech to ACPO conference, 5 October 1989 (text from Home Office).
16. *The Guardian*, 5 July 1990.
17. *The Guardian*, 20 July 1990.
18. Sir Peter Imbert, 'Towards a cost effective service to police the 1990s', Police Foundation Speech, 6 July 1989 (text from New Scotland Yard); summarised in *Police Review*, 14 July 1989, pp. 1416-17.
19. *The Guardian*, 19 January 1990.
20. Alan Eastwood, in *Proceedings of 1989 International Police Exhibition and Conference* (Major Exhibitions and Conferences Ltd, London, 1989), Session 9, pp. 10-16.
21. *Police Review*, 1 July 1988, pp. 1382-3.
22. Roger Birch, *Policing Europe in 1992*, address to Royal Institute of International Affairs, 19 April 1989 (text from Sussex Police).
23. House of Commons Home Affairs Committee, *Practical Police Co-operation in the European Community*, Session 1989-90, 7th Report, Vol. II (HMSO, 1990), pp. 146-7.
24. *Ibid.*, p. 157.
25. *Police Journal*, January 1990, pp. 13-21.
26. Frans Geysels, 'Benelux, the forerunner of the European Community in the field of the free movement of persons across internal frontiers?', *Police Journal*, Vol. 63, No. 2, p. 118.
27. H. Boge, in *Proceedings of Kangaroo Group Conference*, November 1989 (Kangaroo Group, c/o National Westminster Bank, Threadneedle Street, London).

28. Malcolm Anderson, *Policing the World* (Clarendon, 1989), p. 30.
29. *Ibid.*, p. 187.
30. *Ibid.*, p. 188.
31. *Ibid.*, p. 193.
32. *Ibid.*, p. 194.
33. Richard Norton-Taylor, *In Defence of the Realm? The Case for Accountable Security Services* (Civil Liberties Trust, 1990), p. 75.
34. John Newing, in *Proceedings of 1989 Police Exhibition and Conference* (Major Exhibitions and Conferences Ltd, London, 1989), Session 10, pp. 1-14.
35. John Alderson, 'Free movement of persons: open borders and national security', in *1992: One European Market?* (European University Institute, Florence, 1988), pp. 303-8. See also: John Alderson, *Human Rights and the Police* (Council of Europe Directorate of Human Rights, Strasbourg, 1984).
36. See the Green Paper *Extradition*, Cmnd. 9421 (HMSO, 1985).
37. James Morton, *The Criminal Justice Acts 1987 and 1988: A Commentary* (Waterlow, 1988), p. 65.
38. House of Commons Home Affairs Committee, *Practical Police Co-operation in the European Community*, Session 1989-90, 7th Report, Vol. II (HMSO, 1990), p. 158.
39. *International Mutual Assistance in Criminal Matters* (Home Office, 1988).
40. National Council for Civil Liberties, Parliamentary Briefing 88/1 (1988), p. 3.
41. *Convention on the Simplification of Extradition Procedures*, draft EPC 19/89 (unpublished).
42. Francis Maude MP, *Hansard*, 29 November 1989, cols 703-4.
43. M. Zagari (rapporteur), *Report on Problems Relating to Combating Terrorism*, A2-155/89; *Official Journal of the European Communities*, C158 (26 June 1989), pp. 394-8.
44. *Explanatory Report on the European Convention on Mutual Assistance in Criminal Matters* (Council of Europe, 1969).
45. Douwe Korff, *The Diplock Courts in Northern Ireland: a Fair Trial?* (Dutch Institute for Human Rights and Amnesty International, 1984).
46. Sylvia Paisley, *A Guide to EEC Law in Northern Ireland* (Faculty of Law, Queen's University, Belfast, 1986), pp. 156-7.
47. Colm Campbell, *Modern Law Review*, Vol. 52 (1989), pp. 585-621.
48. *Ibid.*, pp. 607, 613.
49. *The Guardian*, 7 April 1990.

50. Michael Zander, *New Law Journal*, 6 April 1990, pp. 474-6; Colm Campbell, *Fortnight*, April 1990, pp. 10-11.
51. Sir Peter Imbert, speech to 11th meeting of chiefs of police from European capitals, Oslo, May 1989 (text from New Scotland Yard).
52. *The Guardian*, 8 March 1989.
53. House of Commons Home Affairs Committee, *Practical Police Co-operation in the European Community*, Session 1989-90, 7th Report, Vol. II (HMSO, 1990), pp. 177-80.
54. *Ibid.*, Vol. I, paras 145-6.

CHAPTER FIVE

Social Europe

The European Community has always paid lip service to the idea of a social dimension to the single market. In this it has acknowledged the lead given on a wide range of human rights issues by the Council of Europe (see below and Chapter Six). Articles 117 to 122 of the Treaty of Rome list 'social provisions' on which member states agree; they include the need to promote improved working conditions and the principle of equal pay for equal work, without discrimination based on sex (Article 119). This latter item is fairly unequivocal and has led to slow but progressive advances, though much remains to be done. In addition, Article 118 charges the European Commission with promoting co-operation in the following fields:

- employment;
- labour law and working conditions;
- vocational training;
- prevention of occupational accidents and diseases;
- occupational hygiene;
- rights of association and collective bargaining.

Until the advent of the Single European Act, the only reference to the enforcement of binding reforms in these areas was in Article 121; this allows the Council to give the Commission 'tasks in connection with the implementation of common measures', with the important restriction that a unanimous decision is required. This meant (and in many areas still does) that one member state can block any form of action. All too often this member state has been the United Kingdom.

The Single European Act inserted two new items (Articles 118a and b) into the part of the Treaty of Rome dealing with social provisions. The first concerns health and safety, and allows the use of 'qualified majority voting' (see Chapter One) to issue binding Directives; the second urges the Commission to 'develop the dialogue between management and labour at European level' with a view to promoting 'relations based on agreement'.

The scene was thus set for a debate which revealed stark differences in philosophy between the British Government and its EC partners, and also produced an unexpected realignment of British politicians; the Conservative Government emerged as a fierce opponent of closer European integration, while opposition parties became increasingly united in singing its praises.

Two main features have emerged from proposals made by the Commission. They were outlined in a speech made by the Commission President, Jacques Delors, to the 1988 TUC conference in Bournemouth.[1] The one which has attracted most publicity is what has become known as the Social Charter (though this is not its full title), and much of this chapter is devoted to it – with most emphasis on women's rights – because it relates to a number of civil liberty issues; the National Council for Civil Liberties (Liberty) includes in its Charter of Civil Rights and Liberties a 'freedom from discrimination on such grounds as disability, political or other opinion, race, religion, sex, or sexual orientation', and some (but not all) of these issues are addressed by the Social Charter.

The other main proposal by the Commission has been raised at intervals since 1970 and has consistently been blocked by the British Government: the idea of a European Company Statute in which worker participation plays an essential part. This continues to produce near-apoplexy among some British employers, although it is increasingly seen as a crucial element of a modern democratic system in other European countries. It is discussed here as part of the pattern of Britain's response to Community policy on social matters.

Development of the Social Charter

The Economic and Social Committee, ECOSOC (a consultative assembly comprising representatives of employers, workers and interest groups such as consumers), has repeatedly asserted that the completion of the internal market should not undermine basic social rights and insisted on the parallel need to foster social cohesion as well. It therefore responded with alacrity when asked by the Commission in November 1988 to draw up an assessment of the possible components of a Community Charter of Basic Social Rights. In February 1989 ECOSOC adopted an Opinion which listed all the basic social rights that member states might be assumed to support, given their inclusion in international charters and conventions drawn up by the United Nations, the International Labour Organisation (a UN agency) and the Council of Europe; it referred in particular to the European Social Charter adopted by the Council of Europe in 1961 (which Britain has ratified), together with a 1988 Additional Protocol which increased its scope.[2]

After February 1989 events moved with accelerating speed. The first draft of a Community Charter of Fundamental Rights was published in May 1989 and put to the Social Affairs Council (comprising ministers for this area from each EC state) in June 1989.[3] Eleven member states broadly welcomed the Charter but Britain did not; Margaret Thatcher had already denounced it as 'a throwback to a Marxist period, a class struggle period' and 'more like a socialist charter'.[4] After discussion at the Madrid summit meeting of the European

Council (also in June 1989), the Charter was revised and considered again by various 'ad hoc' groups as well as the Social Affairs Council.[5]

In an attempt to achieve unanimous endorsement of the Charter at the next summit meeting at Strasbourg in December 1989, French President François Mitterand (who was then also President of the Council) introduced further changes to the draft.[6] One of the more striking alterations was the deletion of a specific reference to a minimum wage. However, Britain still voted against the draft; the only effect of the changes was to infuriate trade union organisations and the European Parliament, which objected to the watering down of the proposals without further consultation. Members of the left-of-centre majority in the Parliament got their own back by delaying a different set of proposals put to them by the Commission during early 1990.[7] Unfortunately the damage had been done, and workers throughout the Community lost some potential benefits.

Scope of the Charter

After a preamble which lays down a set of broad principles (not all of which are mentioned again) the revised Charter defines itself as a Community Charter of the Fundamental Social Rights of Workers.[6] The words 'of workers' did not appear in previous drafts; the change is significant in view of some of the alterations to the text – for instance, the substitution of 'worker' for 'citizen' in the sections guaranteeing equal rights to freedom of movement and social protection. In addition, the term 'worker of the European Community' has been taken in Community law to exclude workers who are resident in the EC but who are not EC nationals (see Chapter Two), so the detailed provisions of the Charter do little for such workers. Another casualty of re-drafting was the disappearance of a specific reference to a *minimum* income for persons unable to enter or re-enter the labour market.[8]

The Charter as adopted lists social rights under the following headings:

- freedom of movement;
- employment and remuneration;
- improvement of living and working conditions;
- social protection;
- freedom of association and collective bargaining;
- vocational training;
- equal treatment for men and women;
- information, consultation and participation for workers;
- health protection and safety at the workplace;
- protection of children and adolescents;
- elderly persons;
- disabled persons.

The Charter was accompanied by an Action Programme listing measures which the Commission regarded as urgent and achievable before the end of 1992.[9] The document is careful to refer to the principle of 'subsidiarity' under which the Community acts collectively only 'when the set objectives can be reached more effectively at its level than at that of the member states'; thus some features of the Charter do not figure in the Action Programme but are left for individual member states to decide. The Commission promises consultation with the European Parliament, the Economic and Social Committee and the two sides of industry; it also urges the Council to make up its mind on the proposals within two years at the latest (i.e. by the end of 1992).

It should be emphasised that the Charter was never intended to be a legally binding document, since it is no more than a general declaration of intent together with proposals for specific measures. Some, but not all, of these are to take the form of binding Directives; in each case there will have to be approval either by unanimity or by a qualified majority (see above and Chapter One), depending on which Article of the Treaty of Rome is invoked as an authority for action. The absence of unanimous support bodes ill for the success of some of the proposals, since Britain in particular may well try to block them. A great deal of ingenuity is likely to be exercised by the Commission in selecting a suitable 'treaty base' in each case, and disputes may have to go to the European Court of Justice.

A Difference of philosophy

The failure to agree over the Charter reveals the extent to which Continental thinking on social affairs and industrial relations has diverged from that in Britain, and this will be discussed in detail under each heading below. At this stage it may simply be remarked that the policy of the British Government over the last ten years has made the collision inevitable.

The Government's opposition to various parts of the Charter, and to comparable provisions at home, has been justified on the basis of the need to compete economically with other countries. This was spelt out by Eric Forth, the Minister for Industry, when he opened a CBI conference in February 1990 on Japanese investment in Britain:

> Britain has one of the lowest labour costs in the European Community – one half of the costs in Germany and one third of the costs in France or Italy. Only Greece, Portugal and Spain are cheaper. The workforce is also skilled and flexible, since it is not limited by rigid labour laws.[10]

The underlying thinking was expressed even more bluntly by the right-wing philosopher Roger Scruton, in a provocative but apparently serious polemic against the idea of spending any more money on education. In support of a plea to lower the school-leaving age he put it thus:

> We must recuperate yet another Victorian value: that of child labour... If the pay were sufficiently low (and children are willing to work for quite paltry sums) there would be no lack of employers ready to offer it. Some might call this 'exploitation'. But why use so rude a word to describe the process which liberates the child from his oppressors, and makes him a useful member of society?[11]

It is hardly surprising that high-wage countries like West Germany (which incidentally set great store by education and training) do not intend to allow Britain to compete on these terms. It also seems unlikely that relatively poor countries like Portugal joined the EC with the idea of remaining less prosperous than the majority, simply in order to compete in the internal market. The philosophical divide has become very deep, but there has so far been little attempt to inform the British public of this debate.

Women's rights

The Action Programme for the Social Charter proposes a third Community programme on equal opportunities for women, to follow the second such programme which runs to the end of 1990.[12] The latter was mainly a set of exhortations to member states, together with pledges by the Commission to collect information, set up networks and study groups, support training schemes, organise conferences and issue guidelines. The few proposals for binding Directives met with little success, as we shall see below.

However, the earlier programme established the clear principle that equal opportunities are not simply a matter of eliminating discrimination against women in employment; women with children or dependent relatives will remain heavily disadvantaged and limited in their options until greatly improved support is available as of right in a wide range of areas – maternity leave, parental leave, leave for family reasons such as a sick child or dependant, childcare services and so on.

Apart from a new equal opportunities programme, the Social Charter Action Programme proposes two non-binding Recommendations: one on childcare, and one on a 'code of good conduct for the protection of pregnancy and maternity'. The only proposal for a binding Directive explicitly directed at women concerns the protection of pregnant women at work. This comes under the heading of health and safety for which a unanimous vote is not required.

Equal pay and equal treatment

The Action Programme proposes nothing directly related to equal pay. It notes with regret that a proposed Directive on social security that would include equality of retirement ages remains blocked (by Britain). However, this proposal was welcomed by a House of Lords Select Committee, which urged the Government to announce a timetable for equalising the state pension ages.[13] Recent rulings of the European Court of Justice will also increase the pressure on Britain to equalise pension ages; the Court ruled, for instance, that occupational pensions (in the private sector) are part of an employee's pay, and must therefore comply with Article 119 of the Treaty of Rome requiring equal treatment for men and women.[14]

Two Directives issued in the mid-1970s were supposed to guarantee equal pay for work of equal value (No. 75/117) and eliminate sex discrimination in access to employment, promotion, vocational training and working conditions (76/207); a third Directive (79/7) dealt with certain aspects of social security.[15] The first of these was important in clarifying the term 'equal work' in Article 119 of the Treaty of Rome; it interpreted this as 'the same work or... work to which equal value is attributed', allowing comparison between non-identical jobs.

However, several member states had to be taken to the European Court of Justice before they agreed to pass adequate national legislation (as required under all Directives). Britain has frequently been taken to the Court by the European Commission, resulting in changes to the Equal Pay Act 1970 and the Sex Discrimination Act 1975. Amendments to the equal pay legislation (incorporating the equal value concept) came into effect in January 1984, and a new Sex Discrimination Act was passed in 1986.[16] Individual cases have also been taken to the European Court with the support of the UK's Equal Opportunities Commission.[17]

The European Commission remains dissatisfied with the level of compliance by many countries with these Directives, and the Action Programme promises an examination of 'remedies and procedures'. This is likely to mean rather more proceedings against member states under Article 169 of the Treaty of Rome, which empowers the Commission to go to the Court after issuing a 'reasoned opinion' and obtaining no compliance within a set period.[18]

Two proposals for Directives appeared in the Action Programme under the heading 'improvement of living and working conditions', and a third under 'employment and remuneration', which if passed seemed likely to benefit women in particular. The aim of all these proposals was to benefit workers who at present have little legal protection: those who do 'atypical work' such as part-time and casual workers, homeworkers, and many who currently work in what is known as the 'black economy'.

These proposals were subsequently split up and recast in a different form, so that at least two of the new proposals could be given a 'treaty base' not requiring unanimous approval by the Council. In June 1990 the following three proposals were announced, though the texts had still not been finalised:

- A Directive demanding that part-time and temporary workers be given rights equal to those of full-time workers in a number of areas: equal access to training and other benefits provided by employers, equal consideration when workers' representative bodies are set up, and opportunities to apply for full-time posts when these are available. This Directive would require unanimous support under Article 100 of the Treaty of Rome.
- A Directive requiring that part-time and temporary workers be given equal benefits (in proportion to hours worked) regarding paid leave, dismissal allowances and seniority allowances; also a demand for legislation setting an overall limit of 36 months to the renewal of 'temporary employment arrangements' (short-term contracts) lasting 12 months or less for a given job. This proposal was submitted under Article 100a (as a measure essential to the 1992 process), which does not require a unanimous vote.
- A Directive (not specified in the Action Programme) to ensure that any short-term contract specifies the nature of the job: qualifications required, place of work, working hours, and in particular any special risks involved. In the last case there is to be special training if required. This measure was proposed under Article 118a (health and safety) which again does not require unanimity.[19]

A further proposal on work contracts in general, particularly important to part-time and temporary workers, was expected late in 1990.

The reaction of the British Government to these proposals was not favourable; they were denounced by the Employment Secretary as 'deliberately designed to discourage part-time work', and government lawyers were said to be preparing a challenge to the chosen 'treaty base' in the European Court of Justice.[20] The explanatory document accompanying the proposals shows that in 1988, the proportion of part-time and temporary workers in the UK had reached 22.8% of all employees – the third highest figure among member states, representing about 36% of all the part-time employees in the Community.[19]

Sex discrimination and the burden of proof

A long-standing problem in sex discrimination is the effect of indirect discrimination – 'where an apparently neutral provision, criterion or practice disproportionately disadvantages the members of one sex, by reference in particular to marital or family status, and is not objectively justified by any necessary reason or condition unrelated to the sex of the person concerned.'[21] Common examples include the following:

- discrimination against part-time workers (who are mostly women) regarding working conditions, career prospects, eligibility for bonuses and allowances, selection for redundancy;
- physical strength requirements;
- age bars which effectively prevent women from returning to work after a break taken to bring up a family;
- conditions related to family responsibilities which operate either against women (excluding those with such commitments) or in favour of men (by giving benefits to those with a 'dependent family');
- requirements of geographical mobility which discriminate against those looking after dependants at home;
- discrimination related to personal qualities or 'acceptability', where this conceals a bias against women;
- discrimination on grounds of pregnancy.

As a general principle of the law in most member states, the person bringing a case of complaint is required to provide the proof. In all but the last of the situations listed above – and even in cases of straightforward, direct discrimination – proving sex discrimination can present the complainant with considerable difficulty, since an employer can always argue that the conditions imposed were justified and not related to gender.

For this and other reasons the Commission took the advice of its expert advisers[22] and proposed a Directive on the burden of proof.[23] The essential feature of this was that the complainant should have to make out only a *prima facie* case to establish a 'presumption of discrimination', after which the employer would have to prove that there was no contravention of the principle of equality. The complainant was to have the benefit of any doubt.

Unfortunately this proposal, like so many others, was opposed in the Council of Ministers by Britain – though other member states such as Ireland and Portugal were known to be glad of the outcome. The modifications proposed by the Council so weakened the draft that the Commission withdrew it altogether, and the matter is back at the level of informal discussions.

Britain objected on the grounds that the Directive would be confusing to apply in the context of UK law – yet Britain's equal pay and sex discrimination laws (which in general compare well with those elsewhere in Europe) already shift the burden of proof to the employer once unequal pay for equal work has been established. In cases of indirect discrimination this happens at the stage where the employer is asked to justify the discriminatory practice; and paradoxically, the Directive would have been most useful in Britain for cases of *direct* discrimination, where some courts have simply accepted the assertion of an employer that the sex of the complainant was not the reason for the action complained of.[24]

Migrant, black and ethnic minority women

The European Commission published a Communication in 1988 which drew attention to the special problems of migrant women.[25] Unlike most Community reports it gives special attention to those coming from outside the Community, and those for whom Europe has long been their home but who come from ethnic minority groups. The report acknowledges that children born in Europe within such groups can suffer the same obstacles as their parents: European women from ethnic minorities 'share problems with women of foreign citizenship, e.g. as regards racial, cultural and sexual stereotypes encountered, and difficulties unrelated to citizenship facing them in their access to training and employment'. Such problems are a common experience of black British women; full citizenship on its own is not enough to prevent this.

The report points out a fundamental problem in assessing the scale of the problems faced by such women: the fact that many of them, although working long hours under oppressive conditions, simply do not figure in the statistics for employment. When working they may be forced for a variety of reasons to resort to the 'black economy', and when unemployed they may not be counted if, for example, they lack work permits and are ineligible for benefits. Research in this field has established, however, that migrant women have a higher rate of 'labour market participation' than non-migrant women in most age groups.[26]

One factor explaining this difference is that migrant women often work full-time for extremely long hours, either for economic reasons or because part-time work tends to be more available in areas such as clerical work where migrant women are under-represented. Despite this fact, migrant women suffer more frequent, and longer, periods of unemployment than other women; the Commission report notes a disturbing trend for this gap to increase.[25]

The Commission report ends with a set of guidelines and a plea for comprehensive action (including special training schemes) to address the needs of migrant women. Perhaps the most important is a proposal to give those who do not already have them a set of *individual* rights to residence permits, work permits and social security. At present, many migrant women are vulnerable to losing their residence status because it is linked to that of a man. Such a reform would also give migrant women a greater degree of mobility in seeking work.

The Commission report promises to 'evaluate the relevant action taken at both national and Community levels in 1992'.[25] There is, however, no proposal in the Social Charter Action Programme that touches on this problem except a general commitment to simplify freedom of movement within the Community. The excuse appears to be a lack of reliable information. The issue is being taken up by the European Women's Lobby (see Chapter Seven) and by the European Parliament's Committee on Women's Rights,[27] and in Britain the Equal Opportunities Commission, the National Alliance of Women's Organisations and the National Association of Local Government Women's Committees are among those actively concerned.

Sexual harassment

This age-old problem has been thoroughly analysed in a report to the Commission by Michael Rubenstein (an editor of the journal *Equal Opportunities Review*), who concludes that existing laws (including those on sex discrimination in the UK) are inadequate because they address the harm only after it has been inflicted.[28]

Although sexual harassment has been accepted as a form of discrimination in the United States, Rubenstein finds that this approach has yet to be adopted by the courts in the majority of EC member states. He argues that sexual harassment should really fall within the scope of the 1976 Equal Treatment Directive 76/207 mentioned above, which in Article 5(1) states:

> Application of the principle of equal treatment with regard to working conditions, including the conditions governing dismissal, means that men and women shall be guaranteed the same conditions without discrimination on grounds of sex.[15]

Drawing on United States case law, Rubenstein argues that sexual harassment should include not only direct physical or verbal approaches but also the use of obscene language and displays of pornography.

A formal declaration by the Community could establish this principle and ensure its incorporation into domestic laws. However, even if the laws of member states were modified in this way it would not tackle the problem at its root (a defect that no doubt applies in the US as well). Rubenstein suggests that the only solution is a Directive along the lines proposed earlier by the European Parliament, embodying positive action 'to ensure ...respect for the dignity of women at the workplace'. His recommendations include the following points:

- Sexual harassment is verbal or physical conduct of a sexual nature which the perpetrator knew or should have known was offensive to the victim [see also below]. It should be unlawful if it can reasonably be claimed that it harmed the victim's working environment. It should also be unlawful if rejection of, or submission to, such harassment is used as a basis for a decision affecting the victim's employment.

- Employers should establish and maintain working environments free of sexual harassment. They should in general be legally liable for failure to do so.
- Those pursuing claims for sexual harassment should be given legal assistance where necessary.
- Measures should be taken to protect employees who submit complaints from any form of victimisation.
- Those who use the judicial process should be protected from unwarranted publicity or intrusion into their private lives.
- Guidance, training and publicity should be used to bring the Directive to the attention of all concerned.

Rubenstein accepts that the definition of sexual harassment must make it clear that the behaviour is offensive to the recipient. However, some women's groups argue that the phrase '...which the perpetrator knew or should have known...' does not go far enough; other recommendations and codes of practice make it clear that the crucial feature is the distress or unhappiness of the victim.[29]

Despite these firm proposals the Commission decided (for reasons not disclosed) not to proceed with a draft Directive that had been prepared, and the Action Programme speaks only of examining 'the protection of workers and their dignity at work'. Under the Irish presidency of the Council in the first half of 1990 there was, however, a formal (but non-binding) Council Resolution on 'the protection of the dignity of women and men at work'.[30] This incorporated most of the recommendations listed above (though not the legal liability of employers), and will at least provide a basis for further proposals.

Pregnancy and maternity rights

The Social Charter Action Programme points out that many past, or currently proposed, measures on health and safety are of particular relevance to women; however, it admits that these may not have taken sufficient account of the specific needs of pregnant women. The Commission therefore intends to propose a Directive on the protection of pregnant women at work, while taking care not to create additional obstacles to the employment of women. Details are still awaited.

A related issue, to be made the subject of a non-binding Recommendation, is the drawing up of a 'code of conduct for the protection of pregnancy and maternity'. This will cover social rather than physical protection: job security, recruitment opportunities, accrued rights and so on. The Action Programme puts it thus:

> If women consider that pregnancy weakens their chances at work, they will be less inclined to have children, and if they want to have children,

> they risk foregoing opportunities for appropriate training. As a result, women will continue to be largely employed in low-level jobs. If they wish both to have a career and children they will have to overcome many difficulties.

The proposal ends on a cautious note with a reference to 'subsidiarity', the principle that 'social protection should be established primarily at national level and the Community should only intervene further if necessary' – a sentiment frequently echoed strongly by the British Government.

Maternity, parental and family leave

The Social Charter declares that measures should be developed 'enabling men and women to reconcile their occupational and family obligations'. However, no specific measures relating to maternity, parental or family leave are proposed in the Action Programme, nor in the Commission's timetable of work for 1990 and 1991.[31]

Britain's statutory provision for maternity leave[32] compares badly with that of its EC partners;[33] in addition there is no statutory provision for paternity or joint parental leave, though some employers have voluntary schemes. Other EC countries offer a variety of statutory rights concerning parental leave, usually available to either parent; they range between a period of unpaid leave (up to three years depending on the country) and paid schemes like that in Denmark, where either parent may take ten weeks at 90% of earnings following maternity leave of 14 weeks at the same rate.[33] There are maternity leave entitlements for homeworkers in Italy, while Germany and Denmark offer leave to care for sick children.[34]

It was recognised at the time of the first Community programme on equal opportunities (1982-5) that parental leave should be one component of such a programme; one of the stated aims was 'to extend parental leave and leave for family reasons',[35] and in 1983-4 the Commission proposed two drafts of a Directive on this issue.[36] The modest aim was that either parent (but not both) should have a right to three months' leave (in addition to maternity leave) to care for a new child, and that workers should have a limited right to time off for urgent family reasons such as the illness of a child or the death of a near relative. However, Britain refused to agree to the proposal and it remains blocked.

In a 1988 report to the Commission by Peter Moss (co-ordinator of the EC's Childcare Network), a new Directive was suggested to cover maternity leave, parental leave and leave for family reasons all together. The main features of this proposal were as follows:

- leave entitlements to apply to all workers regardless of period of service, number of employees in firm or hours of work;
- provision of a minimum of 12 weeks maternity leave plus 12 weeks parental leave per parent (transferable at the discretion of the member state) or 24 weeks for a lone parent;
- provision of a minimum of ten days per year as leave for family reasons for each worker, extended for lone parents and other special cases;
- extension of parental leave over a five-year period to give, when combined with maternity leave, a period of 12 months of post-natal leave available to one or other of the parents following the birth of a child;
- extension, over a five-year period, of benefit payments currently made during maternity leave to cover parental leave as well, with both periods paid at no less than 90% of earnings;
- an option of taking maternity and parental leave in part or overall as part-time leave.[37]

Changes such as these would make a considerable impact in the United Kingdom, where the conditions for reinstatement after maternity leave[32] are so restrictive that almost a half of all employed women do not qualify for a statutory right to return to work.[38] Even the introduction of one component (e.g. paternity leave) would constitute a start; it might break down the widespread misapprehension that such measures are confined to welfare Utopias such as Sweden but are unthinkable in Britain.

Childcare services

The European Childcare Network was set up under the 1986-90 Community programme on equal opportunities.[12] The Network's research shows that in publicly-funded childcare, Britain is once again near the bottom of the league: provision for ages 0-2 caters for only 2% of the age group compared with up to 44% in other member states, while provision for ages 2-5 is 44% compared with up to 95% elsewhere.[39]

There is also a difference in policy associated with this discrepancy. The few public places available in Britain for very young children are generally reserved for those judged by health and welfare authorities to be 'at risk'; there is no attempt to cater for children simply because their mothers go out to work.[40] The UK representative's report to the Childcare Network points out that there are now less than half the number of places for under-fives that existed in 1945.[38] Out-of-school services are largely non-existent in most areas, and a recent attempt by the Government to persuade 30,000 schools to offer out-of-hours childcare (without new funding) produced only seven known schemes.[41] The UK report calls for substantial increases in all childcare services, together with a comprehensive national policy making it a vital ingredient of the equal opportunity programme.[38]

In its 1986-90 equal opportunities programme the Commission undertook to make recommendations for action in the field of day-care facilities with three aims in mind:

- equal opportunities for children;
- freedom of choice for parents regarding family, social and occupational responsibilities;
- demographic impact (i.e. variations in need among different groups).[42]

The Social Charter Action Programme contains no specific proposals in this area apart from promising a formal but non-binding Recommendation (no details specified) which is now expected in 1991;[31] the reference in the earlier document to equal opportunities for children is not repeated. It appears that the Commission wants to carry out more consultation before going further, feeling that the time is not ripe for a Directive (though this was called for by the European Parliament). In view of the likely response from the British and perhaps other governments, this caution is no doubt realistic; it will nevertheless disappoint those who spent so much time assembling information and making proposals.

Positive action

The Action Programme contains no recommendation for action of the kind variously called 'positive discrimination', 'reverse discrimination' or 'quota rules', under which a certain disadvantaged group is given preferential treatment. The Commission's definition of positive action is wider than this; it follows Council Recommendation 84/635 in using the term to cover any measure that helps the cause of equality.[43] Some experts, especially in the British context, make a clearer distinction between positive discrimination and positive action, reserving the latter term for non-quota means of redressing the imbalance between men and women.[44] There are specific provisions for positive action in the UK sex (and race) discrimination Acts involving training schemes and steps to encourage job applications from under-represented groups, but these are much more modest than (for example) the 'affirmative action' programmes in the USA.

The report of the Commission's network of experts on equality issues includes a summary of proposals from the UK members submitted by Christopher McCrudden, one of the British representatives.[22] These do include preferential treatment as well as measures which are ostensibly neutral but designed to assist groups that are under-represented, disadvantaged or discriminated against. The report speaks with approval of the work of Britain's Equal Opportunities Commission, and on the use in Britain of 'outreach' programmes to attract candidates for employment training from under-represented groups. In contrast, the report mentions that the use of quotas for women in local elections has been ruled unconstitutional in France, ironically under the Declaration of the Rights of Man.

Civil rights in the workplace

As mentioned above, there have been three proposals for Directives relating to employment rights, stemming from the Social Charter Action Programme. They cover 'atypical work', i.e. part-time and temporary work. The Action Programme proposes no less than ten Directives relating to health and safety at work, one on the protection of young people from exploitation, and one on improving travel conditions for people with disabilities. However, it offers only a non-binding Memorandum on the multiple disadvantages suffered by non-EC citizens living and working in the Community (see Chapter Two). On fundamental issues relating to union membership the Charter is notably ambivalent: while collective bargaining, arbitration procedures and the right to strike are mentioned, all these rights are subject to 'national legislation', 'national regulations' or 'national practice'.

In the light of what many in Britain see as a steady dismantling of workers' rights by the Government, the Social Charter in its present form seems likely to offer more hope than actual relief from such attrition. The need for relief is illustrated by a European Commission report comparing the rules of member states governing working conditions (contracts, wage regulation, limits on working time, paid leave, dismissal and redundancy, conduct of disputes, information and participation, and collective agreements).[45] On one issue after another the UK appears almost isolated in its inadequate or totally absent protection of workers.

Freedom of association and collective bargaining

The Social Charter as first published[5] contained a number of statements on these topics which were modified or eliminated in the final form.[6] It is worth examining some of the changes because they illustrate what the Charter might have achieved in the absence of British objections; they also explain the anger of members of the European Parliament and others who expected to be consulted.

Both versions embody the principle that a worker has the right to join or not join a union at will, though the wording underwent minor changes. However, a statement in the first version that this right 'shall entail recognition of the right to belong to a union' is missing from the final version. Furthermore, the right to negotiate and conclude collective agreements is qualified in the final version by the phrase 'under the conditions laid down by national legislation and practice'. These changes are clearly relevant to the trend in Britain towards 'de-recognition' of unions by management and the replacement of collective bargaining by individual contracts.[46]

Another significant change is the alteration of a clause specifying the right to strike 'save in exceptions specified in existing legislation.' The final version says: 'subject to the obligations arising under national regulations and collective agreements.' There is also a new clause: 'The internal legal order of the member states shall determine under which conditions and to what extent the rights provided for ...apply to the armed forces, the police and the civil service.' All these changes have a bearing on cases like that of the Government Communications Headquarters (GCHQ) workers in Britain (see below).

The objections of the British Government to the Charter were predictable, in view of its attitude since 1979 to the numerous Conventions drawn up by the International Labour Organisation (ILO), the UN-sponsored successor to the body set up in 1919 to set international standards for working conditions and labour relations. Although Britain had long ago ratified many of the ILO Conventions, in the last ten years the Government has denounced or 'deratified' four of them, most notably the one which requires government contractors to pay fair wages[47] and another relating to minimum wages for vulnerable groups of workers.[48]

Quite apart from this the Government has simply ignored ILO Conventions by which it is still in principle bound. Thus in 1983 the right to belong to a national trade union was withdrawn from workers at GCHQ, despite ILO Convention No. 87 which guarantees workers the right to form and join organisations of their own choosing. The only exceptions apply to the armed forces and the police. The unions took the case to the ILO's Freedom of Association Committee, which ruled unequivocally against the Government; however, the ILO has no enforcement mechanism and the ruling was ignored.[49] A parallel appeal to the European Commission of Human Rights (see Chapter Six) was unsuccessful, on the grounds that the European Convention on Human Rights does not give union rights to 'members of the administration of the state'.[50]

A second major complaint to the ILO arose out of the Teachers' Pay and Conditions Act 1987, which gave the Government the power to impose pay and conditions on teachers, with unions reduced to a consultative role. This was ruled by the ILO to be in breach of Convention No. 98, which deals with the right to organise and conduct collective bargaining.[47] The 1987 Act was supposed to expire in April 1990 in favour of a new, agreed negotiating procedure, but this was not found possible and the dispute remained the subject of discussions between teaching unions and the Government. By mid-1990, however, it seemed likely that agreement would finally be reached, to be followed by new legislation in the 1990-91 session of Parliament.

The ILO has also condemned Britain for breaching its Conventions on a wide range of other issues concerning restrictions on the right to strike and interference in the running of trade unions; it has also deplored the Government's failure to give legal protection to job applicants who are rejected on the grounds of union membership or activity (see below), and its removal of a general right of dismissed strikers to challenge the fairness of their dismissal.[51] However, the erosion of British workers' rights continues.[52]

The only surprise concessions by the Government have been the decision to postpone (though not withdraw) the plan to abolish the national wages councils that have long set minimum standards in the lowest-paid occupations,[53] and the inclusion in the current Employment Bill of a statutory right not be refused employment on the grounds of union membership.[54] This could be interpreted as recognising that the right to join a trade union is (or should be) a fundamental civil liberty. At any rate it may signal a belated recognition of the extent to which Britain is out of step with trends in other EC countries.

Worker participation

Perhaps the most striking divergence between British and Continental practice in labour relations is in the area of worker consultation and participation in decision-making processes. This is increasingly seen in some countries as essential for the just and efficient operation of industry in a democratic society. However, Britain has no formal equivalent of the various mandatory systems of works councils (generally set up on a company basis) which exist in Belgium, France, Greece, West Germany, Luxembourg, the Netherlands, Portugal and Spain.[55] While trade unions may be involved in collective bargaining at national level, the works councils (whose members may or may not be union representatives) are consulted about company policy and plans affecting employment. In West Germany there is also a two-tier system of boards of management and supervisory boards which include worker representatives, quite apart from a framework for industry-wide negotiations between unions and employers.[56]

A system of worker representatives was proposed in Britain in the 1977 Bullock Report, though in this case they were to be part of a single board of management.[57] The idea evoked furious opposition among employers and was criticised for different reasons by many trade unions; the proposal then fell with the Labour government in 1979. In 1980 the European Commission raised the issue again with a draft Directive (the 'Vredeling Directive') which proposed minimum requirements for worker consultation in the larger companies. Specified information was to be supplied to employee representatives at least once a year, and such representatives were to be informed and consulted before the taking of decisions with serious consequences for the workforce.[55]

This modest proposal was, however, blocked by the British Government and work on it ceased in 1983. A similar fate befell the 'Fifth Directive', proposed first in 1975 and revived in 1983, which required the setting up of some form of worker representative body with strict rules regarding the election of members.[56]

A new initiative to overcome British obstruction has involved the revival by the European Commission in 1989 of earlier proposals for a European Company Statute.[58] The main intention behind this is to facilitate the creation of cross-frontier companies by providing an optional model for company structure at the European level which is acceptable to all member states, despite differences between them in matters of company law. (The new type of company would be called a *Societas Europaea* or SE for short.) However, the significance of the proposal in the present context is that it embodies a requirement that employees 'participate in the supervision and strategic development' of the company.[59] Three alternative models are laid down to allow for differing national practices:

- worker representatives on the board (or on the supervisory board in a two-tier system), comprising a third to a half of its membership;
- a separate body of workers' representatives with specified rights to consultation; or
- other models established by mutual agreement, with a 'standard model' as a fall-back to guarantee an equivalent level of participation.

Although these proposals leave important questions unanswered, they clearly offer new developments in the practice of worker participation in the UK.[56] A recent report (by the EC-backed European Foundation for the Improvement of Living and Working Conditions) found that British workers have less say in planning the introduction of new technology in their companies than workers in most other industrialised EC countries.[60]

In correct anticipation of continued opposition by the British Government, the European Commission devised an ingenious division of the proposals into two parts, each of which could be passed by qualified majority voting (see Chapter One) under different articles of the Treaty of Rome (Articles 54 and 101a). However, Britain insists that the correct 'treaty base' for both parts is the article requiring unanimity, and if the proposals are adopted the Government may refer the matter to the European Court of Justice.[56]

Outlawing discrimination

The preamble to the Social Charter contains a general declaration as follows:

> ...in order to ensure equal treatment, it is important to combat every form of discrimination, including discrimination on grounds of sex, colour, race, opinions and beliefs, and... in a spirit of solidarity, it is important to combat social exclusion...[6]

The subsequent text of the Charter and its Action Programme deal with discrimination on the grounds of sex (see above), but other forms of discrimination receive no detailed mention apart from proposals on improving equality of opportunity for people with disabilities.[8] Groups representing people with disabilities appear cautiously optimistic that progress will be made.

Other groups which suffer discrimination have much greater cause for dissatisfaction with the Charter, and we deal with two of these below. The fact that the preamble embraces all forms of discrimination is at least a start; in Continental law (and in the European Court of Justice) such a general declaration carries more weight than it would in Britain.

People with disabilities

The Action Programme emphasises the need to improve equality of opportunity for the more than 30 million Community nationals with long-term physical or mental disabilities. It proposes a five-year Community programme (Helios) to succeed the second such programme which runs to the end of 1991. Such programmes have encouraged EC states to develop pilot schemes for improving the occupational and social integration of people with disabilities, but the Commission points out that a coherent overall policy is still lacking.

The European Parliament has also been pressing for firmer action, specifically in the form of a Directive to ensure that workers with motor disabilities can travel more freely and in complete safety. The Action Programme states that such a Directive will be put forward. Further action is also promised on the Handynet system (exchange of information on technical aids for people with disabilities). There is, however, no proposal actually to outlaw discrimination against people with disabilities.

Race discrimination

The general introduction to the Action Programme stresses the need for member states to eradicate discrimination on the grounds of race, colour or religion 'particularly in the workplace and in access to employment'. This is consistent with the revised description of the Charter which refers specifically to Community workers rather than citizens, but of course it fails to acknowledge the all-pervasive nature of racism and race discrimination in practice. The reality is that, in general, men and women living and working in the Community (regardless of their length of residence), who are not citizens of a member state, have no freedom of movement, cannot vote in local or general elections, and are frequently (as in Britain) legally discriminated against regarding access to certain benefits and services. Neither the Social Charter nor any other policy change currently proposed for 1992 will change this.

The European Parliament has been active for some time in pressing the Commission to draw up firm measures to deal with the problem in all its aspects. In 1985 a Committee of Inquiry reported to the Parliament on the extent of racism and xenophobia in all European countries; it described the activities of fascist and neo-Nazi groups but also went into the widespread prejudices which allow such groups to be tolerated.[61] As described in Chapter Two, this led in 1986 to a Joint Declaration against Racism and Xenophobia (Appendix II) to which the European Council and European Commission as well as the Parliament were party.

Despite this apparently firm commitment, the Commission insists that it has no legal 'competence' under the Treaty of Rome to tackle the problem; the Parliament disagrees, taking the view that a formal declaration of the kind described is tantamount to an addendum to the Treaty. In 1988 the Commission went as far as to propose a formal but non-binding Resolution on racism and xenophobia, together with an action programme including educational measures to promote inter-cultural understanding.[62] However, the Resolution finally passed by the Council in 1990 had been so watered down that Vasso Papandreou, the Commissioner responsible for proposing it, dissociated herself from the wording.[63] Britain was reported to have insisted that the Community had no competence to go further; other Council members agreed that it was a matter for national governments, and pointed to clauses in their constitutions which outlawed discrimination (or in Britain's case, to the Race Relations Act 1976 which has no equivalent in any other member state).

This argument has never satisfied the European Parliament, which in 1989 passed an angry resolution which expressed concern that 'racism and xenophobia are still on the increase in the Community' and drew attention to the severe effects of racial discrimination on immigrants from outside the Community (see also Chapter Two).[64]

Events in 1990 have confirmed this dire prediction with new reports of racist violence in Italy and West Germany, while in France the rise of the Front National (FN) has caused panic among the main political parties.[65] Over seven million people across Europe voted for fascist or far-right groups in the 1989 elections for the European Parliament. The French FN and the comparable Belgian Centre Party, German REP and Italian MSI have between them 20 members of the European Parliament; the FN has 10 members out of the total of 81 from France.

In Britain there have long been complaints of sporadic racial attacks, combined with deep-rooted prejudice and a degree of discrimination that the Race Relations Act has not eliminated. The Commission for Racial Equality points out that there are far too many exceptions to the scope of law enforcement, together with an official policy that is so hostile towards immigrants that it tends to foster racism and discrimination against those already settled here. If there were a firm Community policy on racial discrimination which included equal rights for non-EC citizens settled in the Community, the state of things might well improve.

Though bad enough, the situation is not hopeless; in a 1989 Community-wide public opinion survey on racism, xenophobia and intolerance it was found that eight out of ten people disapproved of the anti-immigration campaigns of racist movements.[66] The European Parliament is clearly determined to keep up the pressure until some action is taken. In July 1990 its second Committee of Inquiry into racism and xenophobia completed a report (drafted by Glyn Ford MEP) for submission to the Parliament in September 1990; this stresses the need for a thorough, continuing analysis of the causes and consequences of racism, coupled with firm action by all concerned – the Council, the Commission and the member states.

The report contains 77 recommendations, among which are calls for equal rights for all EC residents regardless of nationality, including the right to vote and the right to be considered for employment in government service. The committee supports the European Commission's position in favour of Community accession to the European Convention on Human Rights (see Chapter Six), and deplores the fact that the Council has indicated opposition to the idea.

Lesbian and gay rights

Discrimination against lesbians and gay men has also exercised the European Parliament for some time. In 1989 its Committee on Social Affairs, Employment and the Working Environment published a report[67] which was amended by the Parliament to include a recommendation that the Social Charter should ensure the right of all workers to equal protection regardless of a number of factors, including their sexual preference.[68] The European Commission did not include any specific response to this report in the Charter, and this contributed to the rift that developed between the Parliament and the Commission over the drafting of the final version.

The Parliament had already approved a 1984 report by the same committee which urged member states to agree a range of measures giving equal rights to lesbians and gay men:

- abolition of laws against homosexual acts between consenting adults;
- introduction of a common age of consent for heterosexuals and homosexuals;
- a ban on the keeping of special records on homosexuals by the police;
- abolition of the classification of homosexuality as a mental illness;
- outlawing of discrimination in the workplace on the grounds of homosexuality.[69]

As emphasised by a recent survey, all these issues are the subject of wide divergences between the laws and practices of member states, and clearly present problems to lesbians and gay men who wish to exercise their freedom under the Treaty of Rome to move from one EC country to another.[70] As an example, while lesbian and gay couples can enjoy the same legal rights as married heterosexuals in Denmark, they would be open to discrimination or even prosecution in certain other member states. Attempts to get such relationships officially recognised by the Community have so far failed.

The survey shows, however, that official attitudes are becoming more liberal in a number of countries. Two EC countries (Denmark and France) have laws forbidding discrimination against lesbians and gay men, while the constitution of the Netherlands gives protection against any form of discrimination. Comprehensive legislation against such discrimination is being proposed in the Belgian and Dutch parliaments. Laws against public insults and incitement to hatred on the grounds of sexual orientation exist in Denmark and Ireland. In Ireland the law against sexual acts between men was successfully challenged before the European Court of Human Rights in 1988, and the Court ordered the Irish government to decriminalise homosexuality; this is expected within the next two years. Belgium and the Netherlands are considering similar legislation.[70]

Where does Britain stand? The survey finds that the UK has more laws which explicitly, or in practice, discriminate against homosexuals than any other European country, East or West. It also estimates that more lesbians and gay men are prosecuted in the UK for offences relating to their sexual orientation than anywhere else in Europe. The tabloid press is free to fuel popular prejudice against lesbians and gay men. Finally, Britain is unique in having on its statute book the notorious Section 28 of the Local Government Act 1988; this makes it unlawful for local authorities to 'intentionally promote homosexuality' in any way, and forbids 'the teaching in any maintained school of the acceptability of homosexuality as a pretended family relationship'.[71]

The attitude of the European Commission to the issue appears ambivalent. The word 'family', which occurs in the Social Charter in connection with both freedom of movement and equal treatment for men and women, is not defined either to include or exclude homosexual household relationships. The Commission accepts the responsibility to eliminate all forms of discrimination in the workplace, but insists that the Treaty of Rome gives it no clear authority to tackle other forms of discrimination against lesbians and gay men.

There is, however, a blanket provision in Article 235 for action on any Community objective relating to the attainment of the common market, even if the Treaty does not provide the necessary powers. This is, for instance, the legal base for proposals relating to people with disabilities, but Article 235 requires a unanimous decision that is unlikely to be achieved in an area where discrimination through national laws is rife. Lesbian and gay campaigners believe that much more could be done to outlaw discrimination under other sections of the Treaty, and call for work on sexual harassment to cover the harassment of lesbians and gay men on the basis of their sexuality.[72] The recent Council Resolution on sexual harassment (see above) appears to recognise this by referring to 'harassment of both sexes'.[30]

Voting rights

This is an issue of which much more is likely to be heard, as freedom of movement encourages more and more people to cross borders and settle for long periods in another part of the Community. At present, a citizen of an EC state resident in another member state is often no better off than a non-EC national when it comes to exercising voting rights in the country of residence, though the situation varies between countries. Three member states – Denmark, Ireland and the Netherlands – have granted the right to vote in local elections to all residents, including non-EC nationals. Britain is unusual in allowing voting rights in all elections (and the right to stand for Parliament) to Commonwealth and Irish Republic citizens resident here, but the Government strongly resists the idea that this should be extended to citizens of other countries resident here. At the same time, there are moves to register expatriate Britons for voting in UK elections.

The issue was raised by the European Commission when it proposed a Directive on the right to vote; it suggested that all EC nationals should have the right to vote and stand for office in any member state they have been living in for a certain period, though this would apply only to local elections.[73] In evidence to a House of Lords Select Committee, the Home Office disputed the Community's power to legislate in this area. The committee agreed on this point, suggesting a non-binding Resolution instead, but endorsed the proposals in principle as a move to 'reflect the close links between member states'.[74]

We have noted in Chapter Two the strong arguments in favour of giving non-EC nationals resident in the Community the same rights as EC nationals where freedom of movement is concerned. It would be anomalous not to extend this argument to the question of voting rights; if equality of voting rights is considered as desirable for all EC nationals resident in a given member state, then it would be logical to consider non-EC nationals in the same way. The argument is based not so much on 'close links between member states' (see above), as on the need to achieve greater democracy in all the workings of the Community.

Conclusions

The Social Charter will remain the centrepiece of the Community's 'human face' in the immediate future. Its obvious weaknesses should not detract from its importance as a sign of determination by most member states to tackle a wide range of social issues on a Community-wide basis. It is possible to feel some sympathy for the European Commission, which manages to please neither the European Parliament (pressing for more and faster reform) nor the Council, whose members can block, delay or weaken measures put to them without having to justify their actions in public to anyone (including their own national electorates).

There are encouraging signs that the more forward-looking companies may force the pace over the provisions of the Charter. A West German manufacturer opening a plant in Birmingham recently announced that many features of the Social Charter (including worker participation and equal treatment of part-time staff) would be incorporated into a union agreement.[75]

One may ask for how long the rest of the Community will put up with one member (such as Britain) blocking so many proposals for improving individual rights. The reality may be that some member states are not unhappy to see such proposals delayed while more pressing matters (such as the EC's relationship with the new Eastern European democracies) remain unsettled. Ultimately, however, the United Kingdom will in all probability be brought into line, however reluctantly: if not by a specific revision of voting rules, then by the much more far-reaching changes which would be associated with political integration or European Union. This could come sooner than anyone has hitherto thought likely. As shown in Chapter Seven, the run-up to such developments will offer a unique opportunity for social change.

Notes

1. Jacques Delors, *Europe 1992: the Social Dimension* (European Commission Office, London, 1988).
2. *Official Journal of the European Communities*, C126 (23 May 1989), pp. 4-14.
3. COM (89) 248 final (30 May 1989).
4. Quoted later by Tony Blair, *Hansard*, 29 November 1989, col. 727.
5. COM (89) 471 final (2 October 1989).
6. *The Guardian*, 26 October 1989. For full text and a comparison with other international provisions, see: House of Lords Select Committee on the European Communities, *A Community Social Charter*, Session 1989-90, 3rd Report (HMSO, London, 1989), Report Appendix 3. For further analysis, see for example: Lord Wedderburn, *The Social Charter, European Company and Employment Rights* (Institute of Employment Rights, London, 1990); also *Workers' Rights and 1992* (Labour Research Department, London, 1990).
7. *The Guardian*, 14 March 1990.
8. For full texts of the two earlier drafts of the Social Charter, together with resolutions passed by the European Parliament and commentaries from different viewpoints, see *Social Europe*, 1/90 (1990).
9. COM (89) 568 final (29 November 1989).
10. *The Guardian*, 1 March 1990.
11. *Sunday Telegraph*, 11 February 1990.
12. *Equal Opportunities for Women: Medium-term Community Programme 1986-90,* Bulletin of the European Communities, Supplement 3/86 (1986). The first programme ran from 1982 to 1985. For a guide to these and related EC proposals, see *Women and Europe: a Trade Union Guide* (Trades Union Congress, London, 1990).
13. COM (87) 494 final; *Official Journal of the European Communities*, C309 (19 November 1987), pp. 10-13; *European Industrial Relations Review*, Vol. 168 (1989), pp. 2, 25-9; *Equal Opportunities Review*, No. 27 (1989), pp. 15-21; House of Lords Select Committee on the European Communities, *Equal Treatment for Men and Women in Pensions and Other Benefits*, Session 1988-89, 10th Report (HMSO, London, 1989).
14. *The Guardian*, 19 May 1990.
15. For the texts of these and related Directives see *Positive Action: Equal Opportunities for Women in Employment* (Office for Official Publications of the European Communities, Luxembourg, 1988).

16. Angela Byre, *Human Rights at the Workplace* (Policy Studies Institute, London, 1988), pp. 147-75.
17. Sonia Mazey, *Women and the European Community*, European Dossier No. 7, 2nd Edn (Polytechnic of North London Press, 1989).
18. Christopher Docksey, *Social Europe*, 1/88 (1988), pp. 21-6.
19. COM (90) 228 (provisional version of 26 June 1990).
20. *The Guardian*, 14 June 1990.
21. Christopher Docksey, *Social Europe*, 3/88 (1988), pp. 23-31; Angela Byre, *Indirect Discrimination* (Equal Opportunities Commission, Manchester, 1987).
22. Ferdinand von Prondzynski (co-ordinator), *Final Consolidated Report: Network of Experts on the Implementation of the Equality Directives*, V/1087/88-EN (European Commission, Brussels, 1988).
23. *Official Journal of the European Communities*, C176 (5 July 1988), p. 5; for discussion see Christopher Docksey, *Social Europe*, 1/89 (1989), pp. 69-74.
24. *Equal Opportunities Review*, No. 24 (1989), p. 2; Tess Gill, in *Between Equals* (Women's Legal Defence Fund, London), Issue 1 (1989), p. 25.
25. COM (88) 743 final (European Commission, 1988).
26. *The Integration of Women into the Economy* (OECD, Paris, 1985), p. 99.
27. Report by Jane Goldsmith for Anita Pollack MEP (to be published). Summary available from the National Alliance of Women's Organisations (see Appendix III).
28. Michael Rubenstein, *The Dignity of Women at Work* (Office for Official Publications of the European Communities, Luxembourg, 1988). For a summary see: *Equal Opportunities Review*, No. 18 (1988), pp. 38-40.
29. See also: Ann Sedley and Melissa Benn, *Sexual Harassment at Work* (National Council for Civil Liberties, 1984); *Sexual Harassment at Work: a TUC Guide and Workplace Programme for Trade Unionists* (Trades Union Congress, London, 1983); *Industrial Relations Legal Information Bulletin*, No. 398 (1990), pp. 2-11.
30. *Official Journal of the European Communities*, C157 (27 June 1990), p. 3.
31. *CREW Reports* (Centre for Research on European Women, Brussels), February 1990, Annex B.
32. Jean Coussins, Lyn Durward and Ruth Evans, *Maternity Rights at Work* (National Council for Civil Liberties, 1987).
33. Peter Moss, *Childcare and Equality of Opportunity*, V/746/88-EN (European Commission, Brussels, 1988), pp. 56-70. For a shorter version see: Angela Phillips and Peter Moss, *Who Cares for Europe's Children?* (Office for Official Publications of the European Communities, Luxembourg, 1989). See

also: Centre for Research on European Women with James McLoone and Máire O'Leary, *Infrastructures and Women's Employment*, V/174/90-EN (European Commission, Brussels, 1989); Bronwen Cohen, *Structural Funding and Childcare: Current Funding Application and Policy Implications*, V/2267/89-EN (European Commission, Brussels, 1989).

34. Pauline Conroy Jackson, *The Impact of the Completion of the Internal Market on Women in the European Community*, V/506/90-EN (European Commission, Brussels, 1990), p. 9.
35. COM (81) 758 final.
36. COM (83) 686 final; revised draft COM (84) 631 final. Also *Official Journal of the European Communities*, C333 (9 December 1983), pp. 6-8 and C316, 27 November 1984, pp. 7-9.
37. Peter Moss, *Childcare and Equality of Opportunity*, V/746/88-EN (European Commission, Brussels, 1988), pp. 296-7.
38. Bronwen Cohen, *Caring for Children: Services and Policies for Childcare and Equal Opportunities in the United Kingdom* (Family Policies Studies Centre, London, 1989).
39. Peter Moss, *Childcare and Equality of Opportunity*, V/746/88-EN (European Commission, Brussels, 1988), pp. 93-9.
40. *Ibid.*, pp. 102 and 190.
41. *The Guardian*, 14 May 1990.
42. *Equal Opportunities for Women: Medium-term Community Programme 1986-90.* Bulletin of the European Communities, Supplement 3/86 (1986), p. 16.
43. *Positive Action: Equal Opportunities for Women in Employment* (Office for Official Publications of the European Communities, Luxembourg, 1988); Ingrid Christochowitz, *Social Europe*, 1/89 (1989), pp. 65-8.
44. Paddy Stamp and Sadie Robarts, *Positive Action: Changing the Workplace for Women* (National Council for Civil Liberties, 1986); Christine Jackson, in *Sex Discrimination and Equal Opportunity: the Labour Market and Employment Policy*, edited by Gunther Schmid and Renate Weitzel (Gower, 1984), pp. 191-200.
45. *Summary Report on the Comparative Study on Rules Governing Working Conditions in the Member States*, SEC (89) 926 final (European Commission, Brussels, 1989).
46. Lord Wedderburn, *Industrial Law Journal*, Vol. 18 (1989) pp. 1-38.
47. Keith Ewing, *Britain and the ILO* (Institute of Employment Rights, London, 1989), p. 7.
48. Marilyn Taylor, *1992: Whose Europe?* (Greater Manchester Low Pay Unit, 1990).

49. Keith Ewing, *Britain and the ILO* (Institute of Employment Rights, London, 1989), pp. 11-14.
50. Angela Byre, *Human Rights at the Workplace* (Policy Studies Institute, London, 1988), pp. 41-7.
51. John Hendy, *The Conservative Employment Laws* (Institute of Employment Rights, London, 1989).
52. *Clamping Down on Workers' Rights* (Labour Research Department, London, 1989).
53. *Hansard*, 6 March 1990, col. 543w.
54. Mark Hall, *Personnel Management*, March 1990, pp. 32-5.
55. Christopher Docksey, *Modern Law Review*, Vol. 49 (May 1986) pp. 281-313.
56. Lord Wedderburn, *The Social Charter, European Company and Employment Rights* (Institute of Employment Rights, London, 1990). For a recent report on the European Company Statute, see House of Lords Select Committee on the European Communities, *European Company Statute*, Session 1989-90, 19th Report (HMSO, 1990).
57. *Report of the Committee of Enquiry on Industrial Democracy*, Cmnd. 6706 (HMSO, London, 1977); also the White Paper *Industrial Democracy*, Cmnd. 7231 (HMSO, London, 1978).
58. COM (89) 268 final (25 August 1989).
59. Mark Hall, *Federation News*, Vol. 40 (January 1990) pp. 1-9.
60. European Foundation for the Improvement of Living and Working Conditions, *New Information Technology and Participation in Europe: the Potential for Social Dialogue* (Office for Official Publications of the European Communities, Luxembourg, 1989).
61. *Committee of Inquiry into the Rise of Fascism and Racism in Europe: Report on the Findings of the Inquiry* (European Parliament, 1985).
62. COM (88) 318 final; *Official Journal of the European Communities*, C214 (16 August 1988), pp. 32-6.
63. *Official Journal of the European Communities*, C157 (27 June 1990), p. 1.
64. *Official Journal of the European Communities*, C69 (20 March 1989), pp. 40-4.
65. *The Guardian*, 13 April 1990.
66. *Eurobarometer*, November 1989.
67. M. Buron, *Report on the Community Charter of Fundamental Social Rights*, A3-69/89 (European Parliament, 1989).
68. *Official Journal of the European Communities*, C323 (27 December 1989), pp. 44-8.

69. V. Squarcialupi, *Report on Sexual Discrimination at the Workplace*, 1-1358/93 (European Parliament, 1983).
70. Peter Tatchell, *Out in Europe: a Guide to Lesbian and Gay Rights in 30 European Countries* (Channel Four Television, London, 1990).
71. Madeleine Colvin, *Section 28: A Practical Guide to the Law and its Implications* (National Council for Civil Liberties, 1989).
72. *Harmonisation Within the European Community – the Reality for Lesbians and Gay Men* (Stonewall Lobby Group, London, 1990).
73. COM (88) 371 final, amended by COM (89) 524 final.
74. House of Lords Select Committee on the European Communities, *Voting Rights in Local Elections*, Session 1989-90, 6th Report (HMSO, 1990).
75. *The Guardian*, 22 May 1990.

CHAPTER SIX

Human Rights for All

The three Treaties on which the European Community is founded (see Introduction), which together form its 'constitution', do not explicitly mention human rights.[1] Proposals for the insertion of a provision guaranteeing political and fundamental rights were rejected. However, the 1957 Treaty of Rome establishing the European Economic Community requires the recognition of certain rights, as a corollary to the measures taken to attain the common market. As we have seen, it establishes (for example) the right to equal pay for women and men (Article 119). However, in the absence of a mandate from the Treaties or from the member states, the Community does not have and cannot develop a policy on human rights in the full sense of the term.[2] As one commentator has observed:

> Paradoxically the Community has rights without responsibilities: rights to demand that member states create a frontier-free Europe, but no responsibility to ensure that this is done in accordance with [the] protection of Human Rights, [which]... is left to national and international protection machinery.[3]

This is clearly a highly unsatisfactory position for a Community dedicated to a 'people's Europe' without frontiers: why should the legal protection of fundamental international human rights depend upon which part of the Community individuals find themselves in? The need for reform becomes even more pressing in the light of renewed pressure to achieve greater political union (see Chapter One). The more powers the Community acquires, the more crucial it is that these are based on human rights as well as common market considerations; human rights legislation can act as a necessary check on such powers and should, in theory, be encouraged both by those who support and those who oppose European Union.

Community rights and international standards

Human rights have a dual role in relation to the internal market. The Community seems to regard them first and foremost as useful tools for integration; for example, the right to move freely from country to country and to broadcast across frontiers. Less importance is attached to rights as 'weapons in the hands of Community citizens resisting the indignities that might accompany the unbridled forces of the free market'.[4]

The human rights challenge for the Community is not only to ensure that the rights associated with 1992, such as freedom of movement, do not abridge other international human rights, but also to set up effective systems for their protection and enhancement. In addition to general human rights protection in Community law, there is also a need to address the national legislation of each EC country in areas which currently fall outside the Community's jurisdiction.

Before considering how the Community in general and the UK on its own could improve upon their protection of human rights, a distinction should be drawn between *Community rights* and *international human rights*. Many provisions of Community law bestow rights only upon Community nationals. The areas covered often coincide with the subject matter of international human rights: freedom of movement, non-discrimination and so forth. However, generally speaking these Community rights are granted only to Community nationals; unlike international human rights they are *not* 'universal' and granted to all individuals within the territorial jurisdiction of the member states. For this reason (and there are others), it is misleading to equate Community rights with international human rights; nor do Community rights have the same characteristics or status as international human rights.

Community initiatives

Despite the lack of a formal mandate, the Community has taken a number of human rights initiatives since its inception, on the premise that 'the construction of Europe is not only a matter of economics'.[1] The residence rights of Community citizens have been extended, and women's rights in particular have been addressed because the issue is raised (so far as equal pay is concerned) by the Treaty of Rome. Since 1979 members of the European Parliament have been elected by direct universal suffrage. The Community institutions (the Parliament, Council and Commission) have signed two Joint Declarations: a very brief one in 1977, which requires them to respect human rights and fundamental freedoms;[5] and the other in 1986, against racism and xenophobia (see Chapter Two and Appendix II).[6]

In its preamble, the Single European Act (see Introduction) draws attention to the European Convention on Human Rights and the European Social Charter; it regards the rights they enshrine as cornerstones for the construction of Europe, but avoids giving them the status of law. Since 1984 the Secretariat-General of the European Commission has had responsibility for the co-ordination of human rights activities, with a member of the Commission (currently the President, Jacques Delors) in overall charge.

The European Parliament has four committees which draw up reports and resolutions on human rights within the Community: the Committee on Legal Affairs and Citizens' Rights, the Committee on Petitions, the Committee on

Women's Rights and the Committee on Institutional Affairs. The last-named committee prepared the Declaration of Fundamental Rights and Freedoms adopted by the European Parliament (but not the Council) in April 1989 (see below).[7]

The Committee on Petitions receives petitions on a wide range of issues including human rights; in the parliamentary year 1977-8 it received 20 petitions, increasing to 774 in 1989-90. Of these, 68 were classified as coming under the heading of human rights.[8] Broadly speaking, the Committee collects information, forwards it to the petitioner and, in some cases, prepares a report. Although the Committee manages to help some petitioners, it lacks teeth. When MEPs have raised some human rights questions in Parliament, for example telephone tapping and conscientious objection to military service, they have been told that the Community has no competence in these issues.

Defining protected rights

The Community's failure to provide for the systematic legal protection of fundamental human rights is revealed most starkly at the European Court of Justice in Luxembourg. The Court is charged with ensuring respect for Community law. Human rights were originally regarded by the Court as exclusively the responsibility of member states. Since the 1970s, however, a series of judgments has affirmed the existence of fundamental rights for the individual which the Court has inferred from common constitutional traditions among EC countries, and from international treaties ratified by member states.

The most important of these is the Council of Europe's 1950 Convention for the Protection of Human Rights and Fundamental Freedoms, usually known as the European Convention on Human Rights (see below). These fundamental rights are among the general principles of Community law for which the Court must ensure respect. However, the Court has categorically stated that such constitutional traditions remain secondary to EC structures and objectives:

> The protection of such rights, whilst inspired by the constitutional traditions common to the member states, must be ensured *within the framework of the structure and objectives of the Community* [our emphasis].[9]

The international law of human rights, as the Court put it in another case, 'can supply guidelines which should be followed within the framework of Community law'.[10] If internationally accepted human rights are merely 'guidelines', it would appear that Community law is paramount.

Much lawyers' ink has been spilt arguing about the status of fundamental rights, and in particular the European Convention on Human Rights, in Community law.[11] It is certainly the case that the European Court of Justice has referred to the Convention in a number of rulings, but the precise status of international human rights treaties in relation to Community law has not yet been defined. As the European Commission wrote in a formal Memorandum in 1979:

> ...one of the shortcomings affecting the legal order of the Communities [is] ...the impossibility of knowing in advance which are the liberties which may not be infringed by the Community institutions under any circumstances.[12]

Such uncertainty about an entire range of fundamental rights affecting over 200 million people is surely unacceptable. The European Court of Justice certainly considers that it has the task of deciding which fundamental rights are protected by the Community. However, the European Parliament's Committee on Institutional Affairs does not consider this a proper function for the Court. In a 1989 report the Committee said:

> ...it is not the task of the Court to define what constitutes the very essence of a pluralist democracy, i.e. the fundamental rights which must be protected.[13]

Not only is the uncertainty unacceptable, it is also unnecessary. As we shall see, it could be eliminated by the Community enacting a written catalogue of fundamental rights, the course favoured by the Committee on Institutional Affairs.

There is no doubt that some human rights issues fall outside Community law altogether. National measures regulating, for example, the detention and interrogation of suspects or the control of public marches do not fall within Community law. Victims may be able to challenge these measures before national courts or the Council of Europe's European Commission of Human Rights and Court of Human Rights in Strasbourg (see Chapter One), but they cannot challenge them before the European Court of Justice in Luxembourg.

If a Community institution, like the Council of Ministers, violates the European Convention on Human Rights, can victims challenge the institution before the Court of Human Rights in Strasbourg? At present they cannot because the Community is not a party to the Convention. In such a situation the victim can only start proceedings against the Community institution before the European Court of Justice.

In summary, the Community is not adequately equipped to protect human rights:

- its mandate does not explicitly include human rights;

- there is uncertainty as to the scope of the European Court of Justice's protection of human rights;
- while the European Court of Justice has applied the principles incorporated in the Convention on Human Rights in a number of its rulings, the Convention is not *formally* incorporated into Community law;
- proceedings before the European Commission of Human Rights and Court of Human Rights in Strasbourg cannot be launched against EC institutions; and
- Community rights do not have the characteristics or status of international human rights.

The Community's inability to respond effectively to threats to human rights is especially troubling in the context of 1992, and the developments outlined in previous chapters.

A Community Bill of Rights?

Broadly speaking, there are two ways by which the Community could speedily obtain a 'Community Bill of Rights'.

First, the Community could give legal status to the Declaration of Fundamental Rights and Freedoms adopted by the European Parliament.[7] The drafters of the Declaration intended that ultimately the Community's Treaties should be revised to incorporate the Declaration;[14] in the meantime they invited the other Community institutions and member states to associate themselves formally with the Declaration.[7]

The Declaration proclaims a number of civil and political human rights such as the rights to life, freedom of expression, privacy and access to information, as well as economic and social human rights, such as the right to education. It confines itself under Article 25(1) to 'the field of application of Community law'. All the rights set out in the Declaration 'may be restricted within reasonable limits necessary in a democratic society' (Article 26). Some of its provisions, for example freedom of movement, are granted only to Community citizens (Article 8). The right of access to information is limited to documents and data concerning oneself (Article 18). There are no provisions specifically designed for suspects in detention. In terms of content, the Declaration is not comprehensive, but at least it is a step towards a Community Bill of Rights. The drafters of the Declaration argued that it has 'a strong symbolic value': 'with this Declaration, Parliament is demonstrating unequivocally that it attaches prime importance to the protection of the individual.'[15]

A second means by which the Community could obtain a written catalogue of rights is by accession to the European Convention on Human Rights. In

1976 the European Commission declared that it did not consider it necessary for the Community formally to accede to the Convention.[16] In the Memorandum of 1979, however, the Commission changed its mind:

> Closer consideration has recently revealed more clearly to the Commission the disadvantages which arise from the lack of a written catalogue both for the image of the Community in general and for the protection of the rights of the European citizen.[17]

The Memorandum observes that the Convention is only a 'minimum code' and accession would not form 'an obstacle to the preparation of a specific Community catalogue' of human rights.[18] In other words, in the long term it could be followed by a specific Community Bill of Rights (see Chapter Seven). According to the Memorandum, accession would have a number of advantages for the Community. For example, it would improve the Community's image as a place of freedom and democracy. Also: 'accession of the Community to an international mechanism of legal control would underline its own [legal] personality'.[19]

The European Parliament strongly supported the proposal, but nothing further happened at the time.[20] However, the current prospect of forging links with Eastern Europe has prompted a rethink about the need for a Community initiative, and in January 1990 Commission President Jacques Delors announced his intention of proposing accession to the Convention by the Community.[21] Such a step would presumably have to be taken under Article 235 of the Treaty of Rome which requires unanimity.

Lawyers continue to debate the significance of accession. Although no panacea, it would bring specific advantages to the individual. It would not be merely a political declaration of intent such as the 1977 Joint Declaration, but would give individuals legally enforceable rights.[5] Although, as we have seen, it is already the case that the European Court of Justice often looks to the Convention on Human Rights in applying Community law, accession could mean that for the first time, individuals might be able to start proceedings against Community institutions before the European Commission of Human Rights and Court of Human Rights in Strasbourg.

Lawyers also debate what the effect of the Community's accession to the Convention (which in turn would bind all EC institutions) would be on the national law of member states. Would accession amount to back-door incorporation of the Convention into British law? In its 1979 Memorandum, the European Commission argued that it would not:

> Accession by the Community to the ECHR [European Convention on Human Rights] can have implications only for Community law as such.

> Additional obligations would arise only with regard to the freedom of action of the Community institutions and their legislative and administrative functions.[22]

Others have argued differently:

> Accession could mean that national judges would have to consider the Convention (and its case law) when deciding matters covered by Community law.[23]

The second view seems more plausible, and seems to have gained ground more recently within the Commission (see Chapter Three in connection with data protection). In any event, 'accession would mean the Convention exerting a creeping influence on Community law generally'.[24]

Enforcement by Community institutions

Rights flowing from the Treaty of Rome may be enforced not only before the European Court of Justice, but also before the courts of member states.[25] Equipped with an enforceable catalogue of human rights, whether based upon the European Parliament's Declaration or on the European Convention on Human Rights, the Community could then operate a system of judicial review. However, on its own such a system is insufficient. It depends upon victims knowing their lawful rights and having the funds to bring their case to court. In some cases, for example a breach of privacy in relation to personal data, individuals may know the law but be unaware that their rights have been violated. For effective Community protection of human rights, judicial review would need to be complemented by a range of additional measures.[26] Steps would have to be taken to inform potential victims about their rights and how to implement them. Implementation procedures would need to be accessible, and reasonable financial resources available. Some rights might need institutional back-up, as for instance by a Human Rights Commissioner.

At present, five members of the European Commission's secretariat have oversight of human rights activities. Their responsibilities include not only human rights within the Community, but also human rights issues between the Community and third countries. Their work is mainly reactive. What is needed is a dynamic, comprehensive strategy for the protection of human rights within the Community. The current resources in the Commission secretariat devoted to human rights are grossly inadequate for this purpose. A working group could usefully be created with the task of formulating a coherent strategy to tackle the legal and institutional deficiencies in the Community's human rights protection.

Possible elements in a human rights strategy for the Community could include a permanent human rights monitoring and investigation service; Community precedents for such a service are to be found in the fields of anti-dumping and competition. Each Commission service – Environment, Consumer Protection and so forth – might be reorganised so that human rights issues were kept under systematic review. The Commission might appoint one of its number, supported by proper resources, to have special responsibility to scrutinise Community legislation to ensure compliance with international standards of human rights and to actively promote civil liberties in the Community.

The human rights strategy should encompass all Community institutions. Parliament, for example, might amend or reject all human rights proposals which do not include adequate implementation provisions. There have already been several meetings between the European Court of Justice and European Court of Human Rights, but a new human rights strategy might include greater co-operation between the two bodies.

Incorporation of the European Convention into UK law

There is already a consensus among all 12 member states about the appropriate human rights standards. All of them have ratified the European Convention on Human Rights. Moreover, all allow individuals to petition the European Commission of Human Rights (this was introduced in 1966 in the UK), and all accept the jurisdiction of the European Court of Human Rights. However, three member states (the UK, Denmark and Ireland) have declined to incorporate the Convention into their national law as a minimum Bill of Rights.

Incorporation of the Convention into UK law is a widely canvassed proposal which, if implemented, would enhance the protection of civil and political rights in the UK.[27] Not only would it be a step towards harmonisation of human rights standards within the Community, it would also provide individuals in the UK with a weapon to resist the specific national effects of 1992 which fall outside the competence of Community institutions: for example, policy which Britain might develop to extend internal immigration controls should external border controls be abolished. Incorporation is currently the most realistic way for Westminster to enact a Bill of Rights for the UK.

The Convention is an international treaty which the UK ratified, and therefore became legally bound to respect, in 1951. All 23 member states of the Council of Europe (see Chapter One) have now ratified the Convention. It is like a Bill of Rights, but at present it is enforceable by UK citizens only before the European Commission of Human Rights and Court of Human Rights in Strasbourg, and not in the UK courts.

The specific rights protected by the Convention are set out in Articles 2 to 14. They cover the classic civil and political human rights: the right to a fair trial, freedom of thought and religion, and so forth. Apart from the provisions about torture, slavery and the prohibition of retrospective penalties, all of the rights are subject to some qualifications. Since the Convention was originally drafted, eight Protocols have been added to it. The UK has ratified the First Protocol which gives additional rights concerning the peaceful enjoyment of possessions, education and free elections; it has not yet ratified three others, including the Sixth Protocol concerning the death penalty.

Most advocates of a Bill of Rights for the UK agree that the contents of the Convention could be improved. Article 5, for instance, permits the detention of vagrants even if they have not committed a specific offence.

The Convention has established the machinery and procedure for dealing with complaints about alleged violations of its provisions. The procedure is slow, cumbersome and costly. Its inadequacy is a compelling reason to support incorporation, allowing individuals to petition British courts directly. Nearly twice as many complaints have been made against the UK as against any other member state, and in more than two-thirds of these cases the Court of Human Rights has found at least one violation of the Convention.[27]

The judiciary

The Convention on Human Rights, like any Bill of Rights, contains broad and vague phrases: freedom of peaceful assembly, freedom of association with others and so forth. Moreover, most of the rights in the Convention are subject to broad, qualifying phrases. Critics argue that such phraseology gives an inappropriate degree of power on policy issues to unelected and unrepresentative judges, whose outlook may be parochial. However, there are a number of counter-arguments to this view:

- Misgivings about the judiciary could be allayed by judicial reform; for instance, regarding the recruitment and training of lawyers, magistrates and judges. To this end there could be some form of independent judicial appointments committee comprising both professional and lay members.
- The incorporated Convention would not be a substitute for a comprehensive national programme of legislative and administrative reforms providing better protection for civil liberties: for instance, tighter anti-discrimination laws, legislation on freedom of information and right to privacy, guarantees of the right of assembly, statutory safeguards for suspects in detention and so on. These detailed measures would complement the general provisions of the Convention and keep judicial discretion to a reasonable minimum.

- One of the key benefits of an incorporated Convention is that it would educate the public about human rights; the judiciary would not be immune to this process and even if the present generation of judges were to prove resistant to these developments, the next generation might be more receptive.

Effects of the Convention

Despite its unsatisfactory features, many UK cases have been heard in Strasbourg under the Convention. Raising a wide range of important civil liberty issues, the human rights of UK citizens have been extended significantly as a direct result of cases heard in Strasbourg. For instance, because of proceedings under the Convention:

- The Government agreed not to re-introduce interrogation techniques such as sleep deprivation, which had been used in Northern Ireland.
- Mental patients under compulsory confinement now have more rights and a fairer procedure to review their confinement.
- Homosexuality for consenting adults has been legalised in Northern Ireland.
- Corporal punishment in state schools has been abolished.
- No further judicial birchings have taken place in the Isle of Man.
- Prisoners' rights, for instance the right of access to a lawyer, have been extended.
- The laws of contempt, under which a ban was imposed on the *Sunday Times* thalidomide article, were held to be in violation of the Convention and have been amended.
- A judge's order imposing reporting restrictions about a case, or restricting the public's access to court, is now subject to review by a higher court.[27]

In April 1990, the Council of Europe's Committee of Ministers (acting in place of the Court of Human Rights – see Chapter One) ruled in favour of two former officers of the National Council for Civil Liberties (Liberty), Patricia Hewitt and Harriet Harman.[28] It was agreed that MI5, in classifying them as 'subversives' and putting them under covert surveillance, had breached two articles of the Convention on Human Rights: Article 8 which guarantees respect for private life, and Article 13 which demands an 'effective remedy before a national authority' when the Convention has been violated – even when this is done by persons acting in an official capacity.[28]

In total, some 80 UK laws or regulations have been repealed as a result of proceedings under the Convention. Of course, some of the decisions in Strasbourg have disappointed civil libertarians: for example the Government's ban on trade unions at Government Communications Headquarters (GCHQ) was condemned by the International Labour Organisation (see Chapter Five) but upheld by the Commission on Human Rights, which has shown excessive caution in tackling 'national security' issues.[29]

Effects of incorporation

If the Convention were to be incorporated, aggrieved individuals would not have to take their complaints to the European Commission and Court of Human Rights in Strasbourg, but could institute proceedings in the UK courts. Strasbourg would remain available as a final resort to complainants who felt they had not obtained justice in the national courts.

An incorporated Convention, however, would not only apply to cases where individuals instituted proceedings claiming a breach of its provisions. All courts in all cases involving human rights would have to interpret the law in accordance with Convention. The incorporated Convention would thus have an impact on many cases and in all courts, from magistrates' courts to the House of Lords.

Lay magistrates, for instance, often hear cases with a human rights component: the newspaper seller accused of obstructing the highway, the street orator who used insulting words, the picket who ignored the police officer's order to move. In each of these cases, if the Convention were incorporated, the defence could argue that the accused was exercising a legally protected right such as freedom of expression or the right to peaceful assembly. To secure a conviction, the prosecution would have to prove the arrest was 'necessary in a democratic society'. The magistrates' court, when reaching its verdict, would be legally obliged to take into account the accused's rights under the Convention, as well as the limitations placed upon those rights. In contrast, under the current law the accused does not have such legally protected rights for the magistrates to take into account.

A similar situation would arise in the Crown Court, where cases are heard by a judge and jury. In appropriate cases the judge would have to direct the jury on the existence and limitations of rights legally protected by an incorporated Convention, for instance freedom of information and expression. The jury would then have to take these rights and their limitations into account when considering the facts and reaching its verdict. This combination of jury trial and legally protected human rights would provide a protection of civil liberties which is wholly appropriate in a democratic society.

In other words, the incorporated Convention would be integrated into the whole machinery of justice. Its application would depend upon the higher judiciary, lay magistrates and juries.

The advantages of incorporation

The UK is bound to secure everyone in its jurisdiction the rights and freedoms found in the Convention (Article 1). As we have seen, the human rights Commission and Court in Strasbourg have found numerous discrepancies between UK law and the Convention. If, however, the Convention were incorporated into our national law, it would help to ensure that the UK conformed to its international obligations under the Convention.

Incorporation would provide the UK's constitutional and legal system with an explicit and positive recognition of basic human rights. It would also save complainants considerable time and money by enabling them to obtain direct redress from inferior UK courts, recourse to Strasbourg still being available as a last resort.

As an additional advantage it would facilitate the harmonisation of the legal protection of human rights throughout England, Wales, Scotland and Northern Ireland, as well as the rest of the Community, so that the basic rights of the individual would not depend upon where the individual was born or resides.

Incorporation would compel UK legislators, administrators, police officers and members of the judiciary to be concerned systematically and consciously with human rights. Police officers, for instance, would have to be trained not only in police powers, but also in human rights. Judges would have to grasp human rights concepts which, at present, are not found in our law.

Finally and perhaps most importantly, incorporation would educate the public about human rights. An incorporated Convention could be taught in schools as a part of courses on human rights and responsibilities (as is the Bill of Rights in the USA). By giving status to civil liberties, the incorporated Convention would also help to generate a tradition of human rights awareness which is presently lacking in the UK. Public awareness of human rights is the best safeguard against the abuse of power.

In summary, existing legal safeguards in the UK against the abuse of power are less comprehensive and effective than in many, if not all, member states of the Community. Unlike countries with a written constitution and Bill of Rights, our rights are generally defined negatively: we deduce our entitlements from an absence of laws prohibiting them. An incorporated Convention would provide some of the legal definitions and safeguards which are currently lacking, and would help to resist any further erosion of our civil liberties.

Furthermore, incorporation is a more politically realistic goal (at least in the short term) than obtaining agreement on a new and comprehensive Bill of Rights. Because 1992 could accelerate the decline of at least some civil liberties in the UK, the need for incorporation has never been greater. If the British Government were to take this initiative, it would further the harmonisation of human rights standards within the Community.

Conclusions

The Community cannot provide systematic protection for human rights unless its mandate is extended. Without an enforceable, written catalogue of fundamental rights and freedoms, civil liberties within the Community will remain uncertain and vulnerable. The Community needs to prepare its own catalogue of freedoms – a Community Bill of Rights to confront issues like discrimination against non-EC nationals under Community law – and in the meantime adopt the Declaration of Fundamental Rights and Freedoms or the European Convention on Human Rights.

If human rights protection in the Community is to be effective, the enactment of a Community Bill of Rights will have to be complemented by additional measures, such as the appointment of a well-resourced Human Rights Commissioner. First, however, a dynamic human rights strategy for the Community must be formulated.

At the same time, steps must be taken to improve the protection of civil liberties at the national level. Particularly where Britain is concerned, this should involve the incorporation of the European Convention into national legislation as an essential addition to the other harmonisations taking place throughout Europe.

Notes

1. *The European Community and Human Rights*, European File 5/89 (Office for Official Publications of the European Communities, Luxembourg, 1989).
2. The European University Institute, Florence, has undertaken a research project on 'Human Rights and the European Community: Towards 1992 and Beyond', under the direction of Professor A. Cassese. The research team prepared a series of reports published by the Institute in October 1989, including: A. Cassese, *General Report*; Andrew Clapham, *Introduction: An Assessment of the 'Acquis Communautaire'*; J. Weiler, *Methods of Protection*. These were summarised in: A. Cassese, A. Clapham and J. Weiler, *1992 – What are our Rights? An Agenda for a Human Rights Action Plan*, Working Paper LAW 90/2. Some of this chapter has been drawn from the ideas and information published by this research team.
3. Andrew Clapham, *Introduction: An Assessment of the 'Acquis Communautaire'* (European University Institute, Florence, 1989), p. 58.
4. *Ibid.*, p. 3.
5. *Official Journal of the European Communities*, C103 (27 April 1977), p. 1.
6. *Official Journal of the European Communities*, C158 (25 June 1986), pp. 1-3.

7. *Official Journal of the European Communities*, C120 (16 May 1989), pp. 51-7.
8. V. Reding (rapporteur), *On the Deliberations of the Committee on Petitions During the Parliamentary Year 1989-90, with Indications as Regards Future Procedure for Handling Petitions*, Document A3-107/90 (European Parliament, 1990).
9. *International Handelsgesellschaft*, case 11/70 (1970) ECR 1125 at 1134.
10. *J. Nold* v. *Commission*, case 4/73 (1974) ECR 491.
11. The UK's view on this issue has been presented as follows: 'The United Kingdom's view, in general, is that while the validity of a Community act may be assessed against the background of the Convention as an agreement to which member states subscribe, and while such an act may be qualified or even overridden by fundamental principles... which are clearly inconsistent with it, this is not to suggest that every principle established by the Convention constitutes a fundamental principle to which the Community must necessarily be subject.' From Home Office Memorandum, *The European Convention on Human Rights and its Relationship with the Law Derived from the Treaty of Rome*, quoted by Andrew Clapham, *Introduction: An Assessment of the 'Acquis Communautaire'* (European University Institute, Florence, 1989), p. 22.
12. *Bulletin of the European Communities*, Supplement 2/79 (1979), point 5.
13. K. de Gucht (rapporteur), *Report on the Declaration of Fundamental Rights and Freedoms*, Document A2-3/89, Part B (European Parliament, 1989), p. 7.
14. K. de Gucht (rapporteur), *Report on the Declaration of Fundamental Rights and Freedoms*, Document A2-3/89, Part B (European Parliament, 1989), pp. 15-16.
15. *Ibid.*, p. 11.
16. *Bulletin of the European Communities*, Supplement 5/76 (1976), point 28.
17. *Bulletin of the European Communities*, Supplement 2/79 (1979), point 6.
18. *Ibid.*, point 8.
19. *Ibid.*, point 16.
20. *Official Journal of the European Communities*, C304 (22 November 1982), pp. 253-4. The Parliament also called for action on the teaching of human rights in the Community; *ibid.*, pp. 255-6.
21. Jacques Delors, *Address to the European Parliament*, 17 January 1990 (text from the European Commission).
22. *Bulletin of the European Communities*, Supplement 2/79 (1979), point 8.
23. A. Cassese, A. Clapham and J. Weiler, *1992 – What are our rights?* (European University Institute, Florence, 1989), p. 61; see also Andrew

Clapham, *Introduction: An Assessment of the 'Acquis Communautaire'* (European University Institute, Florence, 1989), p. 39, n. 84.

24. A. Cassese, A. Clapham and J. Weiler, *1992 – What are our rights?* (European University Institute, Florence, 1989), p. 61.
25. Peter Oliver, *Modern Law Review*, Vol. 50 (1987), pp. 881-907.
26. The same is true in relation to human rights protection at the national level. The UK, though it lacks a written Constitution, has some (albeit flawed) devices in place, such as the Commission for Racial Equality and the Equal Opportunities Commission. Here we consider additional measures at the Community, rather than national, level because they have received relatively scant attention hitherto. Of course, if implemented their effects would be felt in all member states, including the UK.
27. See, for example: Peter Wallington and Jeremy McBride, *Civil Liberties and a Bill of Rights* (Cobden Trust [now Civil Liberties Trust], 1976); *A Bill of Rights: Why the European Convention on Human Rights should be Incorporated into UK Law*, Briefing No. 13 (National Council for Civil Liberties, 1989); Peter Thornton, *Decade of Decline: Civil Liberties in the Thatcher Years* (National Council for Civil Liberties, 1989), pp. 93-6. Incorporation is a principal demand of the Charter 88 campaign. The idea was also strongly supported in a recent House of Lords debate; see *The Independent*, 24 May 1990.
28. *The Guardian*, 26 April 1990.
29. Richard Norton-Taylor, *In Defence of the Realm? The Case for Accountable Security Services* (Civil Liberties Trust, 1990).

CHAPTER SEVEN

The Case for a Civil Liberties Lobby

This book is based on the premise that the 1992 process, in all likelihood, is irreversible and realistically should be accepted as such in Britain, whatever misgivings may remain about the wisdom of having originally joined the Community. Among current members of the EC, such reservations have persisted longer in Britain than in any other country except Denmark.[1] The British Government has consistently opposed proposals, accepted by other member states in principle, which the Government regards as threats to its sovereignty.

However, many observers argue that in some areas national sovereignty was actually sacrificed many years ago under the terms of the Treaty of Rome, and further ceded under the Single European Act which the Government signed as recently as 1986. Whatever one's views on this question, it has unfortunately diverted attention from other important issues thrown up by the 1992 process, including many concerning civil liberties and human rights. If an acceptable balance between communal benefits and individual rights and freedoms is not achieved now, in the run-up to 1992, it may take a long time to put right.

The Brussels lobbyists

The issue of sovereignty appears to be of little concern to large companies and trade associations seeking to reap the economic rewards of operating on a Community-wide basis. They have accordingly been quick to perceive the advantages of moving with the tide of Community legislation, and attempting to influence it to their advantage. To this end well-funded lobbying operations have been established in Brussels, and are in this sense part of the fabric of the EC. Trade unions are also represented by a European organisation which is similarly active.

In addition, the two sides of industry are well represented on the Economic and Social Committee (ECOSOC) which has a consultative role in the process of Community decision-making (Chapter One). Of the 24 British members of ECOSOC (holding office until September 1990), eight represent the interests of employers and seven those of workers. The remaining nine, classed as 'various interest groups', cover farmers, consumers and the professions. Consumers now have a further input through a Consumers' Consultative Council set up by the European Commission. However, within ECOSOC no member officially represents a human rights organisation or a civil liberties group. Moreover, only five out of the 24 ECOSOC members are women, and only one of these is listed in a directory of members' interests as being connected with a women's organisation.[2]

In one area – that of data protection – commercial organisations have aims which coincide with those of civil liberty campaigners, since they have no desire to see confidential commercial data leaking out because of inadequate Community-wide protection (Chapter Three). The interests of migrant workers from outside the EC have also been taken up by some trade union organisations (usually at the behest of their black members), on the grounds that exploitation is inexcusable whatever the nationality of the worker. On the whole, however, there is a lack of powerful representation for many of the issues covered in this book.

Groups not covered by the established lobbies thus start with a double handicap: they have no formal input to the decision-making process, and since most of them are chronically short of funds, they are unable to match the lobbying of more powerful groups. It is estimated that in numbers alone (not to mention level of funding), the lobbies for the profit-making sector have a 100 to one advantage over non-profit making organisations.[3] Experience suggests that only by setting up international bodies or collaborating with other, like-minded organisations can non-government agencies hope to redress the balance. Such co-operation has been successfully achieved in two areas – the environment and third world development.

Women's organisations have recently made progress in this direction. The idea of the newly-established European Women's Lobby was first discussed 13 years ago at a meeting of Belgian, French and Italian feminists. The organisation now has a formal structure and Community funding; it agreed to hold its first general assembly in September 1990, with four delegates attending from each member state. With a base in Brussels and links with national organisations in each country (such as the National Alliance of Women's Organisations in Britain), it is well-placed to make its voice heard at both national and Community levels.

Under-represented groups often need advice on lobbying, and this has recently been recognised by the setting up of the Brussels-based Euro-Citizen Action Service (see Appendix III). It offers its subscribers office facilities and a documentation centre in Brussels, as well as advice (including legal advice) and information about EC activities.[3] A well-organised lobby also needs to have the resources to monitor all aspects of the legislative process (see Appendix IV).

We have noted throughout the book the relative lack of attention paid so far to the civil liberties implications of 1992. This may be at least partially a reflection of the absence of a civil liberties lobby comparable to those representing other issues or groups.

Issues of concern

What issues might a Community lobby for civil liberties take up? The topics covered in this book, together with specific suggestions or recommendations, are summarised below – but there are of course others that are beyond the scope of this book.

The democratic deficit

This issue (discussed in Chapter One) is in many ways central to the whole debate about civil liberties after 1992. The present framework of the Community offers no equivalent to the system of accountability which operates at national level – where legislation is determined by directly-elected representatives to whom the Government is answerable – yet many powers have already been transferred from national governments to the Community institutions. Power rests with a Council which meets in secret, is outside the control of the European Parliament, and is only accountable to national electorates in the most indirect manner. Its supposed accountability has been rendered even more implausible by the trend towards majority voting in the Council (increased under the Single European Act, and likely to increase further in the future). What remedy is open to a national electorate when its own government is outvoted in the Council?

Even less satisfactory is the delegation of many powers to inter-governmental committees such as the Trevi Group, where far-reaching decisions are taken in the name of the fight against terrorism and drug trafficking. This is the main Community forum for discussing co-operation between police and other law-enforcement agencies – yet because of defects in the Treaty of Rome, the discussions are secret and protected from any form of control by the European Parliament.

The logical answer to such problems is to *amend the Treaty of Rome to increase the power of the directly-elected European Parliament*. At the very least it should have the right to initiate legislation, and should be more meaningfully involved in joint decision-making with the Council. The debate concerning how best to achieve democratic accountability should also extend to the relative powers given to different levels of government – local, regional, national and Community. In this context the Eurospeak concept of 'subsidiarity', whereby decisions are taken at the level most directly affected by them, would come into its own as a guiding principle; it would no longer be invoked solely (as at present) as a defence for maintaining intact the current degree of national sovereignty. It is not meaningful to consider the effects on civil liberties of the 1992 process without entering into this debate on democracy.

Refugees and immigrants

The most glaring defects in the 1992 process appear to lie in its effects on those who are not citizens of an EC state. The way in which issues concerning refugees and immigrants have been handled is a prime example of the consequences of the democratic deficit discussed above. A European Asylum Convention (Chapter Two) has been drawn up by a closed committee of immigration ministers drawn from EC states, with reference to neither national nor European parliaments. Having been signed by the British Government, the Convention will merely be 'laid before Parliament' (without a vote) before it is ratified. Despite the fact that the Convention seems quite likely to make asylum more difficult to obtain, refugee organisations are left with no recourse other than to complain about it once it has come into force.

A further hurdle – the proposed common list of countries whose citizens must obtain a visa to enter the Community – will make it even harder to claim asylum, particularly when combined with 'carrier liability' preventing asylum-seekers from even reaching the frontier (Chapter Two). The latter policy clearly conflicts with the spirit of the Geneva Convention on refugees, which depends for its operation on the right of a refugee to reach a country in order to claim asylum there. The current trend in policy makes nonsense of claims that Europe genuinely seeks to provide a haven for the persecuted, and *the policies of EC states on refugees need to be re-examined for inconsistency with the Geneva Convention.*

Migrants seeking to enter the Community in search of work will face the same restrictive visa policy as asylum-seekers – especially if they are from Third World countries – and this again has been agreed without any form of democratic discussion. In principle there is more hope for third country nationals already resident in the Community, in that their exclusion from the benefits of 1992 is increasingly seen as anomalous; many of them will have made Europe their home for decades. In Britain, some even have a form of British citizenship (British Overseas Citizen or British Dependent Territories Citizen), but the Government has not classed them as full citizens for EC purposes. They are thus excluded from all the benefits of EC legislation – such as freedom of movement – and there is no redress for them at the European Court of Justice.

As in other areas, the European Parliament has led the way here, making the obvious connection between discrimination against 'immigrants' (who may in reality be long-standing residents) and the prevalence of racism in European society. It can be argued that *any Directive giving benefits preferentially to EC nationals and their dependants should be replaced by one that covers all residents of member states.*

Black and ethnic minority groups

Black and ethnic minority groups in Britain and elsewhere are justifiably apprehensive that even those who are citizens of an EC state will suffer after 1992, particularly if the abolition of internal border controls is accompanied by more stringent internal checks (by the police and others) on citizenship and immigration status. Raids on homes and workplaces, and identity checks in public places on non-white people, could all increase as a result.

In the absence of Community-wide anti-discrimination measures, black EC nationals who exercise their right to work in another EC state may find not only that their immigration status is repeatedly checked by over-zealous officials; they may also find it impossible (say) to rent accommodation or to obtain insurance, because of unchecked discrimination in the country to which they have moved. *There is an urgent need for Directives to outlaw racial discrimination in all areas, particularly where it could deter black people from exercising their right to freedom of movement within the Community.* The 'treaty base' for legislation concerning freedom of movement is clear from the Treaty of Rome and the Single European Act.

Unless action is taken on a number of fronts, black groups can continue to argue with justification that in the post-1992 Community, freedom of movement will in reality be available only to one group – white EC nationals. The three other 'classes' – black EC nationals, third country nationals (whatever their length of residence) and refugees – will face varying degrees of restriction.

Information without frontiers

If the movement towards full political union does not lose momentum, one positive outcome could be agreement on a supranational authority to supervise cross-border data transfers. However, in this respect something must be done immediately about a situation that is fast getting out of control. The European Convention on data protection was drawn up long before the current explosion in information technology, and even if adopted by all EC states (which has not yet happened) it would be inadequate to deal with all the problems. The draft proposal for a Directive on data protection (Chapter Three) is a move to address this issue, but it remains to be seen whether the Council will delay or weaken it.

Those in most need of protection are individuals – from asylum-seekers to trade union activists – who may suffer from the unregulated circulation of personal data concerning them. In particular, there is no agreement between EC states on the recording and transmission of 'sensitive data' concerning such things as racial origin, sexual behaviour and political opinions. Here *the UK needs to set its own house in order first, and greater safeguards are needed against the holding and disclosing of sensitive data.* Thus *changes need to take place both at national level – to strengthen Britain's data protection laws – and at Community level, to bring about Community-wide enforcement of common standards.*

A further issue – highlighted, though not created, by the 1992 process – is that of regulating the general exchange of data between government agencies. Britain's Data Protection Registrar is well aware of the problem, but is prevented from doing much about it by the limitations of the Data Protection Act. The potential for creating and misusing a vast file of information covering every citizen is always there, since the data can be used to pick out particular groups of people for selective and unwelcome attention. The technology is already available. The Community might be persuaded to legislate in this area, where some national governments (like Britain's) have failed.

A related issue of particular interest in Britain is that of identity cards. The potential for harassment of individuals by the police and other officials would always be there, particularly if they had the power to demand production of the card at any time. Some politicians and leading police officers dismiss these fears as groundless, and remain ready to resurrect the idea as an 'inevitable' consequence of abolishing internal frontiers. Only the British Government's insistence on keeping border controls has kept the argument in the background; if ever it surfaces strongly again, *the case has been made on civil liberty grounds for opposing the introduction of identity cards in Britain.*

Controlling the police

As in some other areas, the 1992 process has sharpened the national debate on a current issue in Britain: the accountability or otherwise of the police. How can one talk about achieving democratic control over cross-border police operations, when the situation at home is still so unsatisfactory? It is this, rather than the prospect of French gendarmes emerging from the Channel Tunnel firing pistols, that demands attention first.

There has been increasing unease in Britain, heightened by the events of the 1984 miners' strike, about the way in which chief constables can act (albeit with the encouragement of the Government) without reference to the police authorities which support their budgets and represent the interests of local electors. In this drift away from even limited local accountability, the role of the chief constables' organisation (ACPO) has been crucial, as the body to which the Government turns for advice and support.

There is also a trend towards setting up national police intelligence units to deal with certain types of crime, and now a national criminal intelligence unit embracing the Regional Crime Squads, not to mention the increasingly powerful police national computer network. There is thus in some respects already a 'national' police force which has never been legally constituted, and which lacks any corresponding accountability to Parliament (Chapter Four).

1992 does not negate the argument for increasing the degree of control over local policing by police authorities, but at the same time *there is a need to strengthen Parliament's control over nation-wide and international police activities*. The House of Commons Home Affairs Committee has now endorsed this view, and called for a review of the whole system of accountability. At present, cross-border policing is discussed in closed meetings of the Trevi Group, while ACPO is also deeply involved in planning for 1992. Quite apart from the European Parliament's exclusion from the proceedings – deplorable as it is in this and other contexts – there is surely a case for giving national parliaments the right to know what is going on and to vet any agreements reached by their respective police forces. At present the information supplied is meagre and control non-existent.

Calls for the setting up of a European police force will need careful examination. Even if a hypothetical Europol did little more than reproduce the 'postbox' functions of Interpol at European level, strict rules on data protection and the handling of sensitive data would need to be laid down. If it were to have powers of investigation or even arrest, the need for accountability would be critical. There are obvious dangers in making it answerable only to the Trevi Group, which itself operates outside Community jurisdiction. *A way would have to found of making a European police force subject to rules on which the European Parliament was at the very least consulted under the current 'co-operation procedure'* (Chapter One).

When there are moves to harmonise UK legislation in such areas as extradition, there is usually a preliminary discussion paper and a Bill for Parliament to discuss. There is a disturbing willingness, however, for the Government to sign away fundamental safeguards (such as the *prima facie* rule in extradition proceedings) in the interests of harmonisation, in a manner which contrasts strongly with its defence of sovereignty in other areas (Chapter Four). *Apparently uncontentious measures for co-operation on issues like extradition and terrorism should be examined in future with a close eye for detail; when governments are anxious to reach agreement quickly, civil liberties may take second place.*

Social justice in the Community

The Social Charter (Chapter Five) has come to symbolise the deep division between the British Government and its EC partners over what the Community really stands for. The Treaty of Rome's prohibition of unfair competition between member states led logically to the formulation of the Charter: it aims to prevent the undercutting of one state's companies by those of another if this is done at the expense of social benefits for workers. The Government opposes the relevant provisions of the Charter with the argument that British companies need to stay competitive to avoid unemployment.

There will therefore almost certainly be continuing confrontation over each new proposal for a Directive arising out of the Charter – yet this is precisely the area of the 1992 process where the potential benefits for equal rights and civil liberties are greatest. *The Social Charter is as vitally important to civil liberties as it is to employment.*

This applies particularly to the many issues relating to women, both in the Charter and in earlier Community legislation. Britain's sex equality legislation has left many areas of discrimination and disadvantage untouched, and the Social Charter at least offers hope for improvement. There are, however, gaps in the Charter; and in some areas, earlier proposals on topics covered by the Charter have long been blocked by opposition at Council level by certain states, particularly the UK. The most obvious problems, and ways of tackling them, are as follows (for details see Chapter Five):

- Women form a disproportionate part of the Community's total of part-time and temporary workers. It is important that they should benefit from the three new Directives proposed by the European Commission (and opposed by the UK Government), so as to give them employment rights more equal to those of full-time workers.
- Women resident in the Community who are not EC nationals are often only able to stay by virtue of a residence status linked to that of a man. As proposed in a Commission report, the answer lies in giving them *individual* rights to residence permits, work permits and social security.
- Sexual harassment has been recognised as a problem within EC competence by the passing of a Resolution on the subject, but only a binding Directive would ensure firmer protection for women and men who suffer from it. To be fully effective, such a Directive would need to extend beyond harassment by superiors and colleagues in the workplace; it should also apply to those providing or receiving goods, services and facilities.
- The provision of maternity, parental and family leave remains uneven across the Community (with Britain comparing badly with most other member states), and a proposal for a Directive on parental and family leave has been blocked in the Council since 1983. There is a need for binding EC legislation in all three areas.
- Childcare is also poorly provided for in some member states (including Britain), and there is scope for legislation to set a minimum level of provision across the Community.

In all these areas, *the Commission should urgently promote proposals to benefit women which have already been formulated, but which have so far failed to be accepted by the Council.*

Worker participation in key decisions at the workplace, which many would argue is a crucial element of a society governed on democratic principles, is another practice which is increasingly taken for granted in Europe, though it is still anathema to large sections of British employers. If they changed their attitudes, the present objections of the Government to such notions would no longer be tenable. *The European Company Statute should increasingly form a focus for debate.*

Perhaps the weakest area of the Social Charter is that of tackling discrimination (other than sex discrimination), where despite a general declaration against it there are few specific proposals. Only people with disabilities are mentioned in detail, and even here it is a matter of 'improving their social and professional integration'. *There is still a lack of EC legislation to outlaw discrimination against people with disabilities.* In particular (as we have seen above), *race discrimination urgently needs to be combated,* whether or not the Treaty of Rome is held to cover it; there is in any case provision for additional issues to be dealt with if there is unanimous agreement between member states. This need takes on an increased urgency with reports of a rise in racist and fascist activity throughout Europe.

Discrimination against lesbians and gay men should also be faced; in particular, the anomalous position in which they are placed when exercising their right to free movement between countries with widely varying laws on homosexuality. On issues such as this there are grounds for supporting the European Parliament in its long-running arguments with the Council and the Commission.

Voting rights

The denial of voting rights to EC citizens who may be long-term residents of another member state is increasingly seen as anomalous in the context of increasing freedom of movement after 1992. *Extension of full voting rights to all long-term residents – whether EC citizens or not – would be a logical consequence of the 1992 process.*

A Community Bill of Rights

The issues raised throughout this book point to the need for a strategy on human rights. This should operate at two levels: *the adoption of a Community Bill of Rights by the European Community, and incorporation of the European Convention on Human Rights into UK law.* The case for a Community Bill of Rights has already been taken up by the European Parliament (but not by the Council), with its adoption of a Declaration of Fundamental Rights and Freedoms. There are also calls for the Community to accede to the European Convention on Human Rights. Neither the Declaration nor the Convention may be strong enough to tackle certain human rights abuses arising out of the application of EC law – for instance, the inherent discrimination against third country nationals – and this indicates, in the long term, the need for a separate Community Bill of Rights.

The significance of this has become all the more apparent with the recent ruling of the European Court of Justice that UK courts can overrule the British Parliament where it contravenes Community law (Chapter Six). The more power the Community as a body has, the more essential it becomes that it is guided by the principles of human rights, and not just by the dictates of the free market. *Proposals for a permanent working party or consultative committee on human rights should be acted upon.* In this regard, *the existence of a co-ordinated Brussels lobby on human rights and civil liberties issues would clearly be valuable.*

Nearer home, the case for the Council of Europe's Convention on Human Rights being incorporated into British law deserves support. People are increasingly coming to realise that in the UK there are few positive 'rights' as such, but only actions which have not been prohibited. Reservations about addressing this issue through a Bill of Rights generally revolve around the power of interpretation this would give to the judiciary; in response, specific proposals are being developed to make the judiciary more representative of society at large.

The ongoing discussion in Britain will have a useful function (whatever the outcome) in preparing the ground for a wider debate about fundamental human rights in the Community. One point needs to be borne in mind in both contexts: no Bill of Rights can anticipate all the applications of its principles that are likely to crop up. It can guide the framing of new legislation, correct defects in past laws, and speed up the resolution of cases where no precedent exists. However, *a Bill of Rights can never be a substitute for specific laws establishing specific rights.*

Recommendations

The main proposals discussed above can be summarised under ten headings:

- amendment of the Treaty of Rome to remedy the 'democratic deficit' and increase the powers of the European Parliament;
- re-examination of Community refugee policy with greater emphasis on the spirit as well as the letter of the Geneva Convention;
- re-evaluation of the common visa list for immigrants – which is ushering in a 'Fortress Europe' – and freedom of movement for third

country nationals resident in the European Community, on a par with EC nationals.

- revision of Britain's data protection laws to prevent the misuse of 'sensitive data' concerning individuals, and enforcement of Community-wide standards of data protection;
- reform of the present system of accountability of the police in Britain, and strict rules for the accountability of any proposed Community police force;
- implementation of all aspects of the Social Charter and 'unblocking' of existing proposals in the social field, particularly those affecting women;
- action to outlaw discrimination of all kinds – especially on grounds of gender, race, disability or sexual orientation – not only in the workplace, but in the Community at large;
- extension of full voting rights to all long-term residents, regardless of nationality;
- adoption of a Community Bill of Rights, incorporation of the European Convention on Human Rights into UK law, and legislation at UK level to improve the protection of specific civil liberties;
- action at Community level to develop a co-ordinated human rights strategy, including a civil liberties lobby which is consulted by the European Commission.

Conclusion

Although the decade has only just started, it is clear that the 1990s will go down in history as a period of rapid and unprecedented change across the whole of Europe. The process initiated within the European Community could lead, sooner than anyone would have guessed only a year ago, to freedom of movement across the whole continent and even to political union – the ultimate dream of the founders of the Community, in which war between states is ruled out by the dictates of economics and dependence on common institutions, rather than by fragile treaties.

History has shown that economic and political integration are not automatically accompanied by social advances. The achievements of 1992 and beyond will be hollow ones if groups of people are deprived of rights and freedoms available to others. There is a need to test proposals in every field against the clear principles laid down in documents like the Universal Declaration of Human Rights, whose articles nearly all begin with the words: 'Everyone has the right...'.

Equal rights, without discrimination, should be the fundamental rule; yet a basic flaw of the Community has always been that its founding treaties confined the benefits of EC membership to citizens – rather than residents – of member states. Sooner or later the Community must remove this restriction, if the pledge of freedom of movement is not to become a mockery.

Finally, whatever shape the future Community takes, its civil liberties horizon should not coincide with its external borders. Creating a 'Fortress Europe' – in which the rest of the world is shut out – is not only impracticable but morally indefensible if the high ideals of the Community are to have any real validity.

Notes

1. Kim S. Petersen, 'Denmark and 1992: why the Danes "drag their feet" – sometimes', in *European Access*, April 1990, pp. 15-16.
2. *Vacher's European Companion & Consultants' Register* (published quarterly by Kerswill, Berkhamsted).
3. *Euro Citizen*, No. 1 (1990) (Euro-Citizen Action Service, Brussels).
4. Eveline Hunter, 'Euro-voice for women', in *The Independent*, 18 June 1990. See also Appendix III for details.

APPENDIX I

Main features of the Palma Document

The principal topics covered are as follows:

1. *Action at external frontiers.* Essential: checks after 1992 and a system of surveillance at external frontiers [1990]; definition of ports and airports as external or internal frontiers [1990]; co-operation and exchange of information between law enforcement and customs [1991]; problems raised by member states' agreements with third countries (e.g. UK and Commonwealth countries) [before end 1992]; combating illegal immigration networks [before end 1992]; information exchange on persons who are 'wanted' or 'inadmissible'. Desirable: checks on passenger movement at ports and airports [in stages by end 1992]; harmonisation of laws on aliens in general and immigration in particular [end 1992].
2. *Action at internal frontiers and inside the territory of the Community.* Essential: study of the abolition of checks on third-country (i.e. non-EC) nationals [end 1989]; bilateral or multilateral re-entry/readmission agreements on third-country nationals [end 1990]; 'off-setting' (i.e. tightening-up) measures on illegal immigration, drug and other illicit trafficking, articles carried by travellers, judicial co-operation, visa policy, right of asylum and refugee status, terrorism, development of a 'common system of search and information', improved information exchange, harmonisation of firearms law [1991-2]; police and customs co-operation in border areas [1992]. Desirable: obligation for foreigners to fill in hotel registration forms [1992].
3. *Drug trafficking.* Essential: encouraging the Trevi Group to devise off-setting measures needed when internal frontiers are abolished [end 1989]; study of desirability of harmonising laws [1992]; co-operation on detection of money transfers and laundering [1992].
4. *Terrorism.* Essential: information exchange 'about the removal of citizens of third countries which represent a possible terrorist danger to security' [1989]; information exchange on known member's of and activities of terrorist groups [1989]; intensified police co-operation on search operations [1989]; on wanted persons, a study 'concerning the removal of citizens of third countries and concerning police surveillance of suspects' [1992]. Desirable: giving the Trevi 1992 Group a permanent secretariat [1990]; study on central collection of intelligence on terrorism [1991].
5. *Visa policy.* Essential: common list of countries whose citizens are required to have a visa [updated every six months]; harmonising of criteria and

procedures for granting visas [decided in 1988]; common list of inadmissible persons and procedure when such a person has obtained a visa [Convention to apply by end 1992]. Desirable: introduction of a European visa [end 1992]; computerisation of information exchange on visa processing [end 1991].

6. *Refugees*. Essential: determination of State responsible for examining an application for asylum [agreed in principle, Convention to apply 1992]; conditions governing movement within the Community while application being examined [1992]; 'recourse to a simplified or priority procedure, according to national legislation, in the case of unfounded applications' [end 1989]; 'acceptance of identical international engagements with regard to asylum' [1992]. Desirable: databank on applications for asylum, refusal to grant visas and forged papers [first half of 1990]; approximation of criteria for granting right of asylum and refugee status.
7. *Deportation*. Essential: determination of member state responsible for removal [1989].
8. *Judicial co-operation*. Essential: ratification of European Convention on Extradition and other agreements on judicial assistance in criminal matters [first half 1989]; improved channels for communicating extradition requests [end 1989]. Desirable: harmonisation of legal description of criminal charges [end 1992]; study of wider judicial co-operation on pursuit of law-breakers and execution of judgments [1992]; Conventions on child abduction and child custody [1989].
9. *Articles carried by travellers*. Essential: action concerning Directives and Regulations on plant health checks, weapons, veterinary checks and protection of rare species [1989-91].

APPENDIX II

The Declaration Against Racism and Xenophobia

This was a joint declaration signed on 11 June 1986. The text is as follows:

THE EUROPEAN PARLIAMENT, THE COUNCIL, THE REPRESENTATIVES OF THE MEMBER STATES, MEETING WITHIN THE COUNCIL, AND THE COMMISSION,

Recognising the existence and growth of xenophobic attitudes, movements and acts of violence in the Community which are often directed against immigrants;

Whereas the Community institutions attach prime importance to respect for fundamental rights, as solemnly proclaimed in the Joint Declaration of 5 April 1977, and to the principle of freedom of movement as laid down in the Treaty of Rome;

Whereas respect for human dignity and the elimination of forms of racial discrimination are part of the common cultural and legal heritage of all the Member States;

Mindful of the positive contribution which workers who have their origins in other Member States or in third countries have made, and can continue to make, to the development of the Member State in which they legally reside and of the resulting benefits for the Community as a whole,

1. *vigorously condemn* all forms of intolerance, hostility and use of force against persons or groups of persons on the grounds of racial, religious, cultural, social or national differences;
2. *affirm their resolve* to protect the individuality and dignity of every member of society and to reject any form of segregation of foreigners;
3. *look upon it as indispensable* that all necessary steps be taken to guarantee that this joint resolve is carried through;
4. *are determined to pursue* the endeavours already made to protect the individuality and dignity of every member of society and to reject any form of segregation of foreigners;
5. *stress* the importance of adequate and objective information and of making all citizens aware of the dangers of racism and xenophobia, and the need to ensure that all acts or forms of discrimination are prevented or curbed.

APPENDIX III

Organisations and Sources of Information

Entries are listed below under chapter headings. In most cases the function of the organisation is evident from its name, and/or it has been cited (at the end of the appropriate chapter) as the source of one or more publications. Only where this does not apply are explanatory notes added.

Chapter One: How the European Community works

European Commission offices in the UK (see also Appendix IV concerning publications):

Windsor House, 9-15 Bedford Street, Belfast BT2 7EG (tel. 0232-240708).
4 Cathedral Road, Cardiff CF1 9SG (tel. 0222-371631).
7 Alva Street, Edinburgh EH2 3AT (tel. 031-225 2058).
8 Storey's Gate, London SW1P 3AT (tel. 071-222 8122; library open to visitors 10am-1pm, telephone enquiries 2pm-5pm).

European Parliament office in the UK: 2 Queen Anne's Gate, London SW1H 9AA (tel. 071-222 0411; library open 10am-1pm, 2pm-5pm).

European Commission headquarters: Rue de la Loi 200, 1049 Bruxelles, Belgium (tel. 010 322 235 1111 for main switchboard; also direct lines to individuals, for which in many cases only the last four digits vary).

Council of Europe: Palais de l'Europe, 67006 Strasbourg, France (tel. 010-3388 614961).

Federal Trust for Education and Research: 1 Whitehall Place, London SW1A 2DA (tel. 071-839 6625).

Chapter Two: Fortress Europe

European Consultation on Refugees and Exiles (ECRE): 3-9 Bondway, London SW8 1SJ (tel. 071-582 9928).

Joint Council for the Welfare of Immigrants (JCWI): 115 Old Street, London EC1V 9JR (tel. 071-251 8706).

Kaamyabi ('Success'): 17 Grange Court, North Grange Mount, Leeds LS6 2BZ (tel. 0532 755272).

Refugee Council (formerly British Refugee Council): 3-9 Bondway, London SW8 1SJ (tel. 071-582 6922).

Refugee Forum/Migrant Rights Action Network: 54 Tavistock Place, London WC1 (tel. c/o ARHAG, 071-482 3829).

Runnymede Trust: 11 Princelet Street, London E1 6QH (tel. 071-375 1496). Organises research, publications and seminars on immigration and race relations.

World Development Movement (WDM): Bedford Chambers, Covent Garden, London WC2E 8HA (tel. 071-836 3672). Campaigns for improvements in UK and EC policies affecting the Third World.

Chapter Three: Information and Big Brother

Data Protection Registrar: Springfield House, Water Lane, Wilmslow, Cheshire SK9 5AX (tel. 0625-53577).

Privacy Laws & Business: 3 Central Avenue, Pinner, Middlesex HA5 5BT (tel. 081-866 8641).
Offers research, publications, advice, training and conferences on worldwide data protection issues.

Chapter Four: Policing Europe

Association of Chief Police Officers (ACPO): Room 1133, New Scotland Yard, London SW1H OBG (tel. 071-230 1212).

Centre for Police and Criminal Justice Studies: University of Exeter, Exeter EX4 4QJ (tel. 0392-411263).

Chapter Five: Social Europe

Campaign Against Racist Laws (CARL): c/o 15 Kenton Avenue, Southall, Middlesex UB1 3QF.

Centre for Research on European Women (CREW): 38 Rue Stevin, B-1040 Brussels, Belgium
(tel. 010 322 230 5158).

Commission for Racial Equality (CRE): 10-12 Allington Street, London SW1E 5EH (tel. 071-828 7022).

Equal Opportunities Commission (EOC): Overseas House, Quay Street, Manchester M3 3HN (tel. 061-833 9244).

European Women's Lobby: c/o Jacqueline de Groote, Avenue de Mercure 11-Bte 4, 1180 Bruxelles, Belgium (tel. 010 322 217 9020).New umbrella organisation.

Family Policies Study Centre: 231 Baker Street, London NW1 6XE (tel. 071-486 8211).

Institute of Employment Rights: 98 St Pancras Way, London NW1 9NZ (tel. 071-482 3892).

Labour Research Department (LRD): 78 Blackfriars Road, London SE1 8HF (tel. 071-928 3649). Trade-union-based research and information service.

National Alliance of Women's Organisations (NAWO): 122 Whitechapel High Street, London E1 7PT (tel. 071-247 7052).

Stonewall: 2 Greycoat Place, London SW1P 1SB (tel. 071-222 9007). Campaigns on lesbian and gay issues.

Chapter Six: Human rights for all

International Centre for the Legal Protection of Human Rights (Interights): 46 Kingsway, London WC2B 6EN (tel. 071-242 5581). Offers publications and advice on human rights to lawyers and non-lawyers, and representation before international tribunals on international human rights law.

Chapter Seven: The case for a civil liberties lobby

Euro-Citizen Action Service (ECAS): 98 Rue de Trone, B-1050 Brussels, Belgium (tel. 010 322 512 9360). Newly formed information and consultancy service for non-government organisations working at international, European, national and regional levels.

Scottish Council for Civil Liberties (SCCL): 146 Holland Street, Glasgow G2 4NG (tel. 041-332 5960).

APPENDIX IV

A Description of the European Lobbying System

There are various guides to lobbying in the UK, and there is no need to repeat here the details given elsewhere.[1] Lobbying at European level is similar in principle to lobbying at parliamentary level in Britain, despite the very different framework of decision-making (see Chapter One).

The European Commission

As in Britain, seasoned Euro-campaigners try to influence decisions at the earliest possible stage by talking to civil servants involved in policy-making. This is even more so in Brussels, where the Commission is officially charged with initiating policy rather than responding to the current government's demands. In one respect they are similar to civil servants in Whitehall: Commission officials have favourite schemes which may fail to get past the Council, and are then put aside to be resurrected at regular intervals. Lobbying by the public on an issue and pressure from MEPs can improve the chances of a proposal the next time it surfaces.

Commission staff, being policy-makers as well as mere functionaries, are perhaps readier than Whitehall bureaucrats to discuss policy with outsiders; they do not have to pretend to have no personal view. In some ways the process of formulating proposals is more open than in Britain, since specialist reports and discussion papers are freely available – provided one knows what to ask for and who is dealing with the issue. For this reason, lobbyists tend to make personal visits to Brussels, and find personal interviews more productive than letter-writing.[2]

Despite the common image of a vast faceless bureaucracy, Commission officials are relatively approachable and not great in number in view of the scope of their activities. According to one writer, the number of executives employed (as opposed to supporting staff such as interpreters and translators) is smaller than in the average British city council.[3]

The European Parliament

Like MPs here, members of the European Parliament (MEPs) expect to get requests for help from constituents and campaigners, though it may be hard to catch them in person while in transit between Strasbourg, Brussels, the London office of the party group and their constituency.

Although the power of MEPs to influence events is very limited at present, they are probably no less effective in practice than their party-whipped counterparts in Westminster. British MEPs are commonly regarded as more independent-minded and willing to take initiatives than MPs at home, and in the European Parliament they sit not in national groupings but in groups of broad political alignment. They tend naturally to take a wider and more European view, which may well conflict with that expounded by the party leader in London. For these reasons they are more open to lobbying.

The lobbying process

Experienced lobbyists say that good initial research and fact-finding is especially useful when lobbying at European level. They find many officials and MEPs to be somewhat understaffed and isolated from developments on the ground, and only too glad to be presented with new facts. In the case of MEPs, this then enables them to confront the Commission with evidence that action is needed.

It needs to be borne in mind that Commission staff, like MEPs, have varying views on a given issue; in particular, where two directorates-general of the Commission are concerned with the same issue, they may not agree as to which is the best policy to propose. For this reason, policy proposals (say, for a new Directive) may undergo a long gestation period within the Commission before they are put to the Council. Lobbyists may thus need to approach more than one official to find out how policy is likely to develop.

Experience has shown that cases need to be put in appropriate Eurospeak terms, and with a knowledge of the limitations imposed by the Treaty of Rome and the Single European Act; for instance, a proposal relating to racism is more likely to make progress if it can be linked with a need to ensure freedom of movement for EC nationals regardless of ethnic origin – the 'treaty base' problem referred to at intervals throughout this book.

Finally, lobbying continues throughout the complex process of decision-making – particularly where the 'co-operation procedure' operates (see Chapter One) – and the final decision may be influenced at any one of several stages of consideration by Commission, Parliament and Council. A proposal which appears to have been successfully launched by initial lobbying may later be stopped in its tracks by counter-lobbying from a different interest group. Lobbyists therefore find that they need to be active at every stage.[4]

Notes

1. See, for example: Des Wilson, *Pressure: the A to Z of Campaigning in Britain* (Heinemann, 1984); Alf Dubs, *Lobbying: an Insider's Guide to the Parliamentary Process* (Pluto, 1988).

2. John Palmer, 'Brussels bogeyman is Thatcher's nightmare', in *The Guardian*, 27 April 1990.
3. For details of Commission staff and their areas of responsibility, see for example *Directory of the Commission of the European Communities* (European Commission, sold through HMSO); *Vacher's European Companion & Consultants' Register* (Kerswill, Berkhamsted); *Dod's European Companion* (Dod's, Etchingham). All these publications are updated regularly.
4. For detailed information on this and related topics, including summaries of Community proposals in various fields affecting the concerns of non-government organisations, see *ECAS Newsletter*, No. 1 (1990), available from Euro-Citizen Action Service, Brussels (see Appendix III). See also: Stanley A. Budd and Alun Jones, *The European Community: a Guide to the Maze* (Kogan Page, 1989); Stephen Crampton, *1992 Eurospeak Explained* (Rosters, 1990).

APPENDIX V

A Guide to Official Publications

Commission and Council documents

Proposals submitted by the Commission to the Council are first published from Brussels in typescript form; they carry a reference number such as COM (88) 376, and may include explanatory memoranda. Draft proposals usually appear later (without memoranda) in the 'C' series of the *Official Journal of the European Communities*. This comes out irregularly – almost every day, and sometimes more than once on the same day – and each issue has a number such as 'C126'. The numbering starts afresh in each calendar year, so the date of issue is also quoted in a reference. Proposals that are finally approved as legislation appear in the 'L' series of the *Official Journal*, and there is an 'S' series for such things as tenders.

Other Commission documents (often the most informative ones) are working documents or discussion documents which may only be available from the offices of the Commission. These have their own numbering system, as in: V/746/88 (published by DG V of the Commission in 1988). There are also glossy journals such as *Social Europe*, which comes out three times a year together with a somewhat confusing range of supplements and special reports. It offers insights into Commission policy on social issues.

European Parliament documents

The European Parliament has yet another system, though it also publishes the minutes of its proceedings (including votes, amendments and resolutions) and answers to written questions in the 'C' series of the *Official Journal*. Its Session Documents (formerly called Working Documents) are published separately, and were split in 1985 into three series: 'A' for reports to the Parliament, 'B' for motions for resolutions and oral questions, and 'C' for documents sent for consultation by the Commission or the Council.

These documents are also coded according to the five-year parliamentary periods of office since direct elections started: '1' for July 1979 to June 1984, '2' for July 1984 to June 1989, and '3' for July 1989 to June 1994. A second part of the code is the serial number, which since 1990 has started afresh with each calendar year; thus A3-1/90 was the first report of 1990. However, in earlier years the serial numbers started at the beginning of the 'parliamentary year' which dates from the first Tuesday in March; thus A2-222/87 was actually published in February 1988.

In addition to minutes published in the *Official Journal*, there is an annex to this journal which publishes the verbatim report of parliamentary debates, translated into each official language; this comes out roughly six months after the relevant session. Before this there is a provisional 'rainbow' version giving a verbatim report of debates in the languages used by the different participants. This has no reference number, but carries the date of the appropriate sitting.

Finally, the bemused researcher may encounter Parliament documents which carry only a number starting with the letters EP. All the Parliament's draft documents are first given such a serial number, and this is retained at the foot of any subsequently published Session Document. However, at this stage the EP number is of no further use in locating it.

Where to obtain documents

Many EC documents may be purchased in the UK from HM Stationery Office, or consulted and copied in the various information offices of the Commission (see Appendix III). They are also kept in the numerous European Documentation Centres (EDCs), which in the UK are mostly based in university and polytechnic libraries. Some of these have a specialist librarian in charge. For a list of the UK's 48 EDCs, see for example *The Europe 1992 Directory: a Research and Information Guide*, edited by Antony Inglis and Catherine Hoskyns (Information Technology Consultancy Unit, London, and Coventry Polytechnic, 1990).

Parliament documents (and some, but not all, Commission documents) are also kept in the European Parliament's library in London (see Appendix III), which will send photocopies of Parliament documents (but not others) by post, if they are not too long.

Unfortunately there is more difficulty with material produced by the Council of Europe which, though it can be purchased from HMSO, is kept by few libraries except on a patchy basis. It may be necessary to write or telephone the Council's headquarters in Strasbourg (see Appendix III) to find out what is available on a given topic.

Index

Civil Liberties Trust Publications

General (Please add 70p per title p & p, orders over £15.00 post free)

1992 And All That: Civil Liberties in the Balance: Michael Spencer (1990) £ 4.50
In Defence of the Realm? The Case for Accountable Security Services: Richard Norton-Taylor (1990) £ 3.95
Application Refused: Employment Vetting by the State: Ian Linn (1990) £ 3.95
Right of Silence: James Wood and Adam Crawford (1989) £ 2.95
The Price of Justice: Howard Levenson (1981) £ 2.95
Drifting into a Law and Order Society: Stuart Hall (1979) £ 0.95
Incitement to Disaffection: Thom Young (1976) £ 1.20

Policing and Criminal Procedure

Troops in Strikes: Steve Peak (1984) £ 4.95
Police Authorities During the Miners' Strike: Sarah Spencer (1985) £ 1.95
Policing the Miners' Strike: edited Bob Fine & Robert Millar (1985) £ 4.95
Controlling the Constable: Tony Jefferson & Richard Grimshaw (1984) £ 7.95

Northern Ireland

Supergrasses: Tony Gifford QC (1984) £ 1.50
Abolishing the Diplock Courts: S C Greer & A White (1986) £ 3.95

Race, Nationality and Immigration

Towards a Just Immigration Policy: edited Anne Dummett (1986) £ 7.95
Black Magistrates: Michael King & Colin May (1985) £ 4.95

Ethnic Minority Language Leaflets (1989):

Making a Complaint Against the Police £1.00 per set (inc. p&p) (individual copies free with an SAE, bulk rates available on request)

Gujarati
Hindi
Bengali
Chinese
Spanish
Urdu
Punjabi

Women's Rights

Women Inside: Silvia Casale (1989) £ 6.95
Judging Inequality: Alice Leonard (1987) £ 9.95

Liberty Publications

Civil Liberty Briefings

(all priced at £1.00 inclusive of p&p)

Police Accountability (1986, revised 1990)
The Conservative Government's Record on Civil Liberties (1987)
Travellers on the Road (1987)
Public Order Act (1987)
The Privacy Implications of the Poll Tax (1988)
The Employment Bill 1987 (1987)
The Official Secrets Act (1988)
The UK Record on Civil Liberties (1988)
Identity Cards and the Threat to Civil Liberties (1988)
A Bill of Rights (1989)
Freedom of Expression in the UK (1989)
Employment and Trade Union Legislation in the 1980s (1989)
Who's Watching You? Video Surveillance in Public Places (1989)
Report on the Security Service Bill (1988)

General

(Please add 70p per title to cover p&p; orders of £15 and over, post free)

Know Your Rights! Factsheets pack (1990) £ 7.95
The Economic League: The Silent McCarthyism: Mark Hollingsworth & Charles Tremayne (1989) £ 3.95
Penguin/Liberty Guide to Your Rights: Malcolm Hurwitt & Peter Thornton (1989) £ 4.99
Section 28: A Practical Guide to the Law & its Implications: Madeleine Colvin (1989) £ 4.50
Decade of Decline: Civil Liberties in the Thatcher Years: Peter Thornton (1989) £ 3.95
Fire Under the Carpet – Civil Liberties in the 1930s: Sylvia Scaffardi (1986) £ 4.95
Stonehenge: NCCL (1986) £ 1.95
We Protest – The Public Order Debate: Peter Thornton (1985) £ 3.95
Trade Unionists & Public Order: Marie Staunton (1985) £ 1.50
Free to Walk Together: Marie Staunton (1985) £ 1.50
The Purging of the Civil Service: NCCL (1985) £ 0.95
Civil Rights for Civil Servants: NCCL (1984) £ 0.95
The National Council for Civil Liberties – The First 50 Years: Mark Lilly (1984) £ 5.95
Gay Workers, Trade Unions & The Law: Chris Beer, Roland Jeffery & Terry Munyard (1983) £ 1.75
Changing Contempt of Court: Andrew Nicol & Heather Rogers (1981) £ 1.20

Policing And Criminal Procedure

No Way in Wapping (1986) £ 1.95

Called to Account – The Case for Police Accountability in England & Wales: Sarah Spencer (1985) £ 3.95
Civil Liberties in the Miners' Dispute (Independent Enquiry Report) (1984) £ 1.50
Poor Law: Ros Franey (1983) £ 1.95
A Fair Cop: Patricia Hewitt (1982) £ 1.75
Southall – 23 April 1979 (Independent Enquiry Report) (1980) £ 2.20
Death of Blair Peach (Independent Enquiry Report) (1980) £ 1.50
Operation Fire/Operation Tan (1980) £ 1.25

Northern Ireland

Enduring Inequality: Religious Discrimination in Employment in Northern Ireland: Vincent McCormack & Joe O'Hara (1990) £ 3.95
The Gibraltar Report – Independent Observer's Report on the Gibraltar Enquiry: Hilary Kitchin (1989) £ 4.00
The New Prevention of Terrorism Act 1984: Catherine Scorer, Sarah Spencer & Patricia Hewitt (1985 updated 1990) £ 2.50
Strip Searching – Women Remand Prisoners at Armagh Prison 1982-1985: NCCL Report £ 1.95

Privacy and Freedom of Information

Privacy and the Poll Tax: Liberty / ALA
Public Information Leaflet (1989) £ 1.00
A Guide to Good Practice for Councillors (1989) £ 2.50
A Guide to Good Practice for Local Government Officers (1989) £ 5.50
The Zircon Affair: Peter Thornton (1987) £ 0.95
Data Protection: Roger Cornwell & Marie Staunton (1985) £ 3.95
Whose File is it Anyway? Ruth Cohen (1982) £ 0.20

Womens' Rights

Maternity Rights at Work: Jean Coussins, Lyn Durward & Ruth Evans (1987) £ 1.50
The Rape Controversy: Melissa Benn, Anna Coote & Tess Gill (1986) £ 1.50
Women Won't Benefit: Hilary Land & Sue Ward (1986) £ 1.95
Positive Action for Women: Paddy Stamp & Sadie Robarts (1986) £ 4.95
Judging Women: Polly Pattullo (1984) £ 0.95
No More Peanuts: Jo Morris (1983) £ 2.50
Amending the Equality Laws: Catherine Scorer & Ann Sedley (1983) £ 0.95
The Equality Report: Jean Coussins (1976) £ 1.20
The Shiftwork Swindle: Jean Coussins (1979) £ 0.60

Race, Nationality and Immigration

British Nationality: Ann Dummett & Ian Martin (1984) £ 2.95
Race Relations Rights: Paul Gordon, John Wright & Patricia Hewitt (1982) £ 1.95

THE CIVIL LIBERTIES TRUST

The Civil Liberties Trust, sister organisation to the National Council for Civil Liberties (*Liberty*), is a registered charity which was established in 1963 to undertake research and education on civil liberty issues.

How You Can Help

The Civil Liberties Trust depends on generous public support for its survival. As a registered charity, the Trust can recover tax from the Inland Revenue on any covenanted donation.

- ☐ I enclose a donation to the Civil Liberties Trust
- ☐ I would like to make a covenant to the Civil Liberties Trust (form overleaf)
- ☐ Please send me information about the work of the Trust
- ☐ Please send me information about joining Liberty

Make a covenant to the Civil Liberties Trust and bring us the one-third you pay in tax.

If you pay tax, there's a simple way of increasing the value of your gift at no extra cost to yourself. If you fill in the form overleaf, we can claim back the tax you have paid, increasing your donation by one-third if you pay tax at the basic rate.

Covenant Form

My name is . . . .

and my address is . . . .

. . . .

. . . .

. . . .

I promise to pay the Civil Liberties Trust £.........every year/half-year/quarter*. My covenant will last for 4 years/7 years*(but will be cancelled if I die sooner). *Delivered under my hand and seal*

Signature . . . .

on . . . . (date).

Please get a friend to witness your signature:

My witness's signature . . . .

Now please fill in the Banker's Order Form

Date . . . . To . . . .

. . . .

. . . .

(Bank name and branch address)

Please pay to the credit of the Charities Aid Foundation (D) account number 36880043 at NatWest Bank Ltd, 126 High Holborn, London WC1 (sort code 60-30-06) for the later credit of The Civil Liberties Trust on...................... (date) the sum of £........... and the same sum on the same date annually/half yearly/quarterly* until 19......... (last year of payment). Please debit my account number.............. accordingly.

Signature . . . .

Name . . . .

Address . . . .

. . . .

* *delete whichever does not apply.*